ALFRED BUCKHAM
DAREDEVIL PHOTOGRAPHER

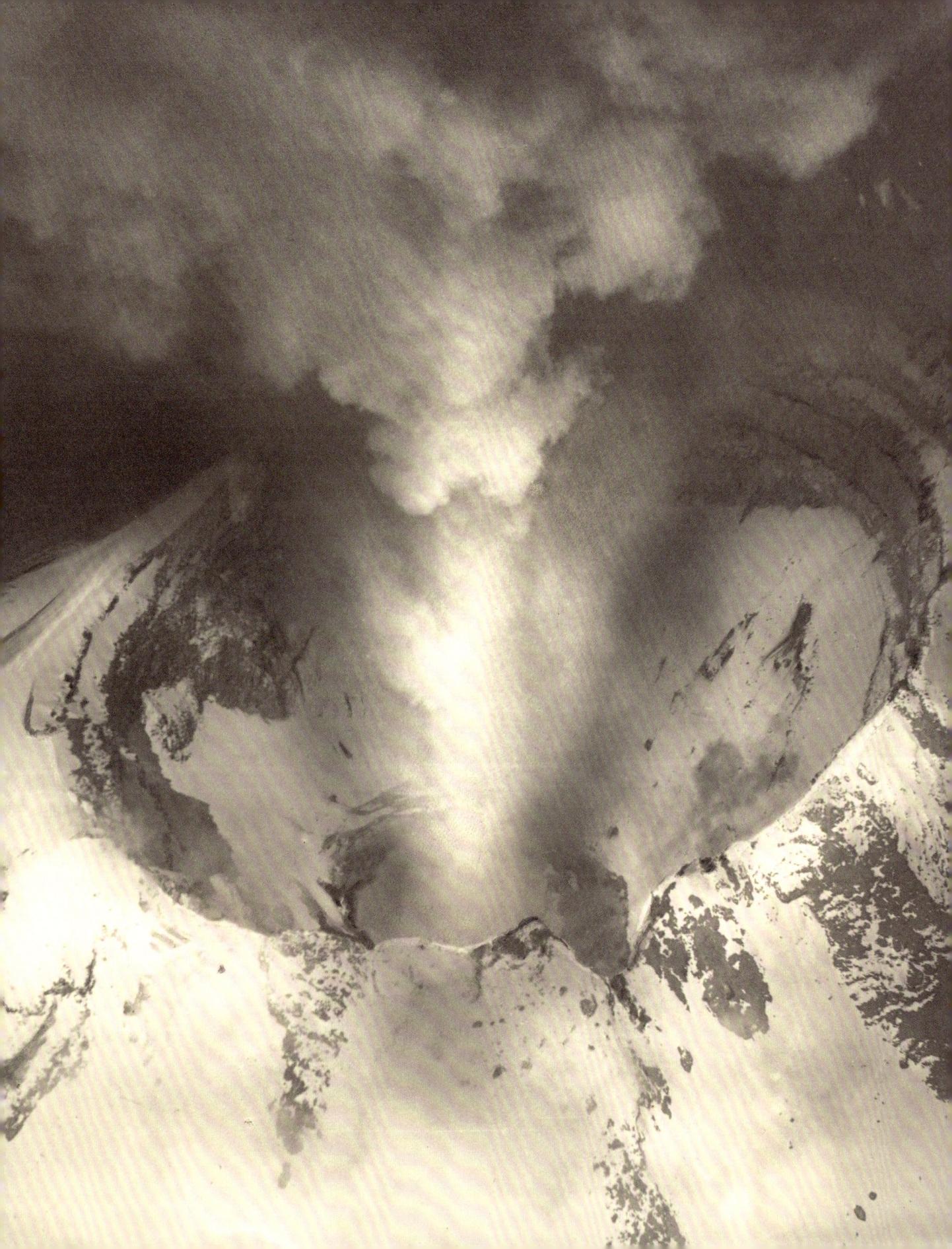

Alfred Buckham
Daredevil Photographer

LOUISE PEARSON

with an introduction by James Crawford

NATIONAL GALLERIES OF SCOTLAND, EDINBURGH

Published by the Trustees of the National Galleries of Scotland to accompany the exhibition *Alfred Buckham: Daredevil Photographer*, held at National Galleries of Scotland: Portrait, Edinburgh, from 18 October 2025 to 19 April 2026.

ISBN 978 1 911054 68 9

British Library Cataloguing-in-Publication Data
A catalogue record for this book is available from the British Library

Project Manager for this title: Jonny Clowes
Copy-editor: Howard Watson
Proof-reader: Susannah Lawson

Publishing Team
Publisher: Ann Crawford
Publishing Project Editor: Catherine Aitken
Publishing Co-ordinators: Jonny Clowes, Megan Boyle
Publishing Assistant: Caitlin Mellon

Designed and typeset by Ocky Murray in Mercury and Founders Grotesk
Printed in Italy by Graphicom

All works are by Alfred Buckham unless otherwise stated.

Picture credits

Cover: *Edinburgh* (detail of 32), *c*.1920

Back cover: *Over the Alps* (detail of 19), *c*.1920

Inside front flap: *Fairey Napier in Flight* (detail of 18), *c*.1930

Front flap quote from 'Masters of photography: Captain A.G. Buckham', *Camera*, January 1927, p.354

Inside back flap: *Where Lightnings Lurk* (detail of 9), *c*.1920

Back flap quote from 'Pictorial photography in the skyway', *Amateur Photographer*, May 1929, p.26

p.2: *Volcano. Crater of Popocatépetl* (detail of 80), 1931

p.6: *Christ the Redeemer, Rio de Janeiro* (detail of 69), 1931

p.8: *Cloud Turrets* (detail of 41), *c*.1918

pp.14–15: *Bristol Fighter in Flight* (detail of 7), *c*.1920

pp.40–41: *Edinburgh Castle* (detail of 35), *c*.1918

pp.58–59: *Winter Treads on the Pentlands* (detail of 51), *c*.1920

pp.72–73: *Botofogo Bay, Rio de Janeiro* (detail of 70), 1931

The proceeds from the sale of this book go towards supporting the National Galleries of Scotland.

For a complete list of current publications, please write to:
NGS Publishing at the National Galleries of Scotland: Modern, 70 Belford Road, Edinburgh EH4 3DE
or visit our website: www.nationalgalleries.org

National Galleries of Scotland is a charity registered in Scotland (No.SC003728).

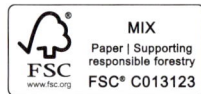

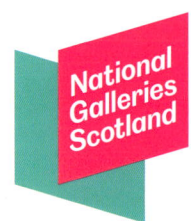

Contents

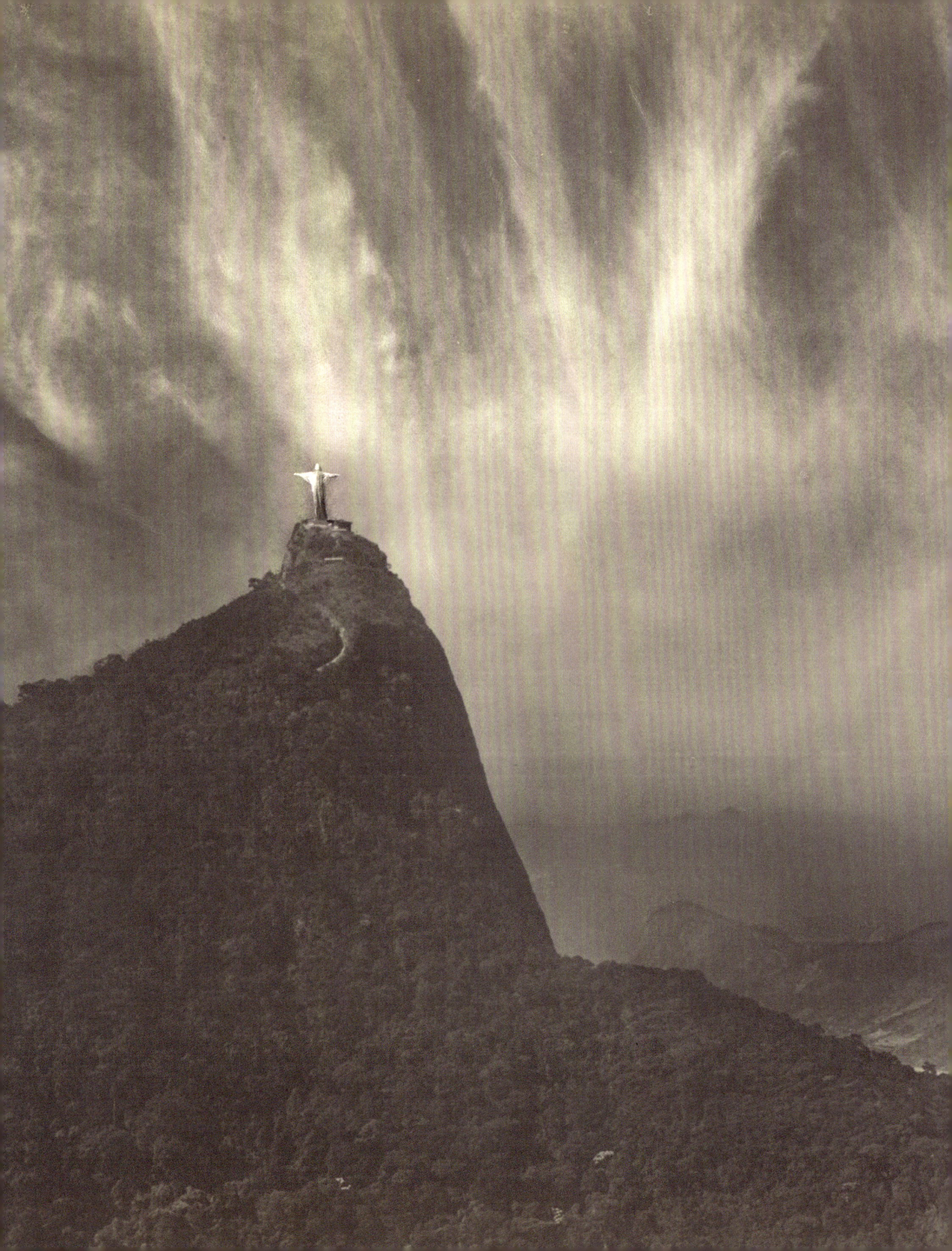

Director's Foreword

ALFRED BUCKHAM'S eye-catching photograph, *Edinburgh* (see page 43), is one of the most popular artworks in the National Galleries of Scotland collection. For residents of the city and visitors alike, it has a star quality that grabs your attention. The photographer makes us feel like we are gliding, weightless and free, above Scotland's majestic capital city. This enthralling image becomes even more intriguing when you learn that it is a darkroom jigsaw – a composite photograph made through a combination of technical skill and creative vision.

The exhibition *Alfred Buckham: Daredevil Photographer* and this accompanying book tell his remarkable story. From wartime aerial reconnaissance photographer to intrepid explorer via many loop the loops, he was a true daredevil. Buckham's plucky character shines through the accounts of his escapades. It is hard not to read these and wish you had heard the tales from the man himself, while simultaneously feeling thankful that you never joined him on a flight.

We are enormously grateful to the Buckham family for their support and enthusiasm for this project. This is the first major exhibition dedicated to Alfred Buckham, made possible by the inclusion of photographs and documents from his extensive archive, which is currently in the care of his grandsons Richard and John. I would like to extend particular thanks to Richard and his wife Maggie for welcoming my colleagues Louise Pearson and James Berry into their home during an extended period of research.

Alongside his family, Buckham has been tirelessly championed by Celia Ferguson, whose publication *A Vision of Flight: The Aerial Photography of Alfred G. Buckham* was the first in-depth study of his exceptional life and work. It is thanks to Celia and Dr Sara Stevenson, the first Curator of Photography at the National Galleries of Scotland, that we find Buckham's photographs in our collection.

Buckham's daredevil spirit has captured the imagination of many colleagues at the National Galleries of Scotland. We are especially grateful for the expertise of Senior Paper Conservator James Berry and Photographer Graeme Yule, whose dedicated investigations mean we know exactly what Buckham was getting up to in the darkroom. After fifty years at the galleries, James is hanging up his flying googles with this exhibition. We are delighted that Buckham's photograph *The Loop* (see page 23) has joined the collection in his name.

I would also like to thank James Crawford, writer and presenter of the BBC series *Scotland from the Sky*, for giving us an insight into Buckham's experience of flight in his brilliant introduction. This publication has been expertly led by Jonny Clowes in our publishing team, and we are grateful for the expertise provided by Stuart Archibald and his colleagues at the Montrose Air Station Museum.

Lastly, we are indebted to Curator of Photography Louise Pearson for her work on the exhibition and publication. Through her skillful handling of both, Buckham is soaring high once again!

Anne Lyden
Director General
National Galleries of Scotland

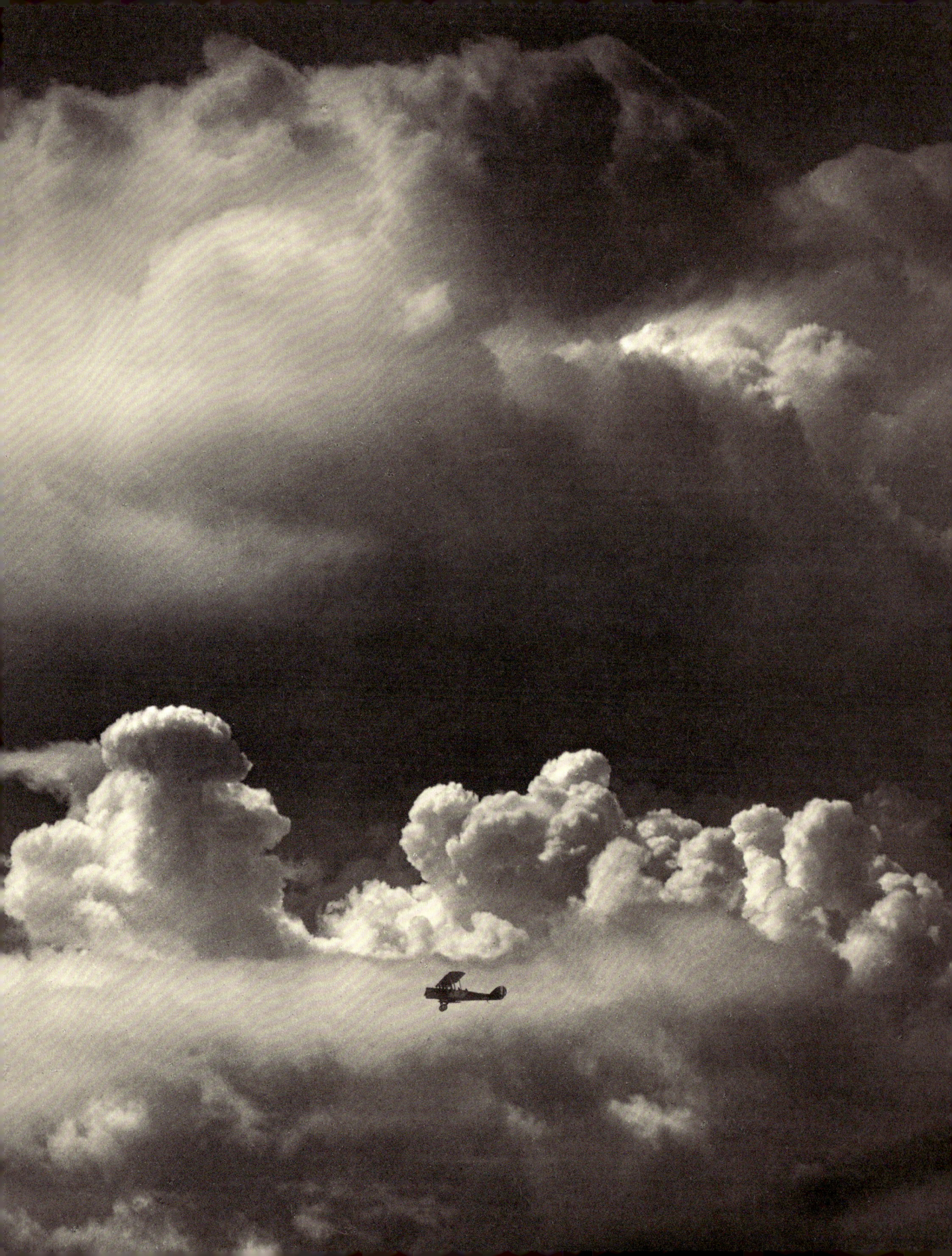

Introduction

James Crawford

OVER THE YEARS, the cloud library grew and grew. There were thin clouds broken by shafts of sunlight. Great, thick accumulations of cumulus clouds pressed together like so many cotton balls (see opposite). Dark and threatening cumulonimbus stacked up into billowing domes and towers. Honeycombed stratus clouds layered like haphazard mosaics. It was an archive of skyscapes that grew to over 2,000 in number and was captured and contained in a series of forty or so cardboard boxes of varying sizes, although most were around 10 by 12.5 centimetres. Some were catalogued with handwritten notes as 'good clouds', others relegated to the discard pile as 'mostly useless'. These boxes moved from house to house in southern England, and, recently, were packed neatly away in a cupboard in a family home in the London suburb of Twickenham. Today, part of the cloud library has travelled north, to find a new home in the collections of the National Galleries of Scotland.

The collector of this cloud library was a man called Alfred Buckham. As revealed in this book, Buckham was a 'daredevil photographer', a 'maverick of early aviation' and a darkroom 'innovator'. Let's add another epithet, either as a statement or a question. Alfred Buckham was an *artist*.

The cloud library was crucial to what Buckham was trying to do: to make the viewers of his images – people then and people now – feel what he was feeling when he was up in the sky. Not *see*, but *feel*. Strictly speaking, the majority of the images that he created were not real. Or at least not real in the sense that he would take his camera up in an aircraft, make an exposure and then faithfully reproduce the results. By and large, had he simply followed that approach, he would have failed in his ambition. He could not, with the technology of the day, have photographed the landscapes beneath him and simultaneously captured the fine detail of the sky. The latter would have been lost, blown out, blank. This, then, was where the cloud library came in. To best represent the sensation, the overwhelming visual overload of being in the air – an experience which, at the time that Buckham first began flying in the early twentieth century, very few had shared – required a dash more creativity.

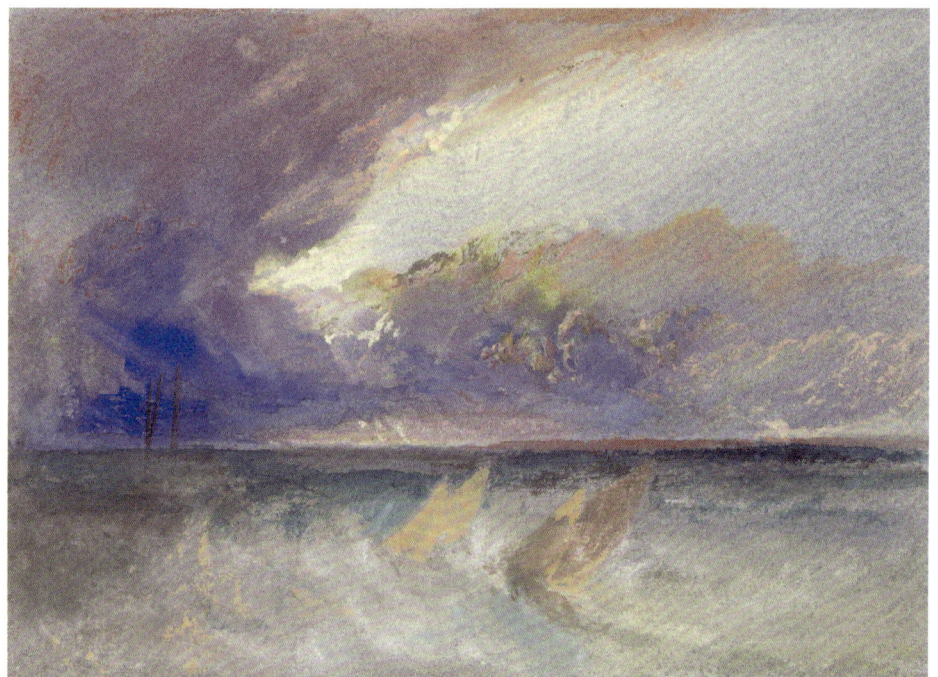

1. Joseph Mallord William Turner
1775–1851, *Sea View*, mid-1820s,
watercolour and bodycolour
on blue paper, 13.5 × 19 cm.
National Galleries of Scotland.
Henry Vaughan Bequest 1900

In his darkroom, Buckham would blend his landscapes together with
just the right selection of images from his cloud library, sometimes even
overlapping negatives to stack clouds one on top of the other. Always
he was attuned to the way the light hit the clouds and the way it hit the
cities or buildings or streets or rivers or mountains below – as he put
it, 'heavy cloud masses insist that they shall have corresponding shapes
upon the earth'.[1]

The darkroom was, in a sense, his artist's studio, the place where he
would mould reality, manipulating his prints as they developed, creating
final images that were far greater than the sum of their parts. Of those
parts, there was one final ingredient. Somewhere between land and sky,
Buckham would also place a third, separately photographed, element:
aircraft. Delicate, fragile-looking open-cockpit biplanes, soaring above
the ground and backlit against the heaped immensity of his clouds.
Ironically, these aircraft (they had their own library, too) were always
photographed while on the ground, to ensure that the images of them
were clear and sharp. Photographing them in flight would have been
near impossible.

Time and again, Buckham would take these three elements –
landscape, sky and aircraft – and combine them in images that are
consistently breathtaking. While still a young man, Buckham aspired

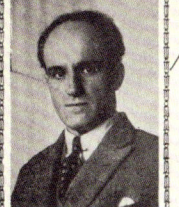

to be a painter, and was drawn in particular to the works of the great Joseph Mallord William Turner (1775–1851, see opposite). He shared Turner's fascination with the magical qualities of light, and the grandeur – sometimes seductive, sometimes terrifying – of nature. For me, in the composite photographic images that Buckham came to produce, there is a kind of aerial sublime that echoes clearly the spirit of Turner. There is no other word for this effect, I think, than *artistry*.

Buckham was not concealing his techniques or presenting his imagery as documentary – he was open and fulsome about his process, its technical difficulties and its challenges. Negatives and prints were the brushes he worked with, stitching and blurring land and cloud and sky and aircraft together. It is, of course, the point of art to elicit feeling, to manipulate reality to hint at deeper truths. Yet it can also indulge and revel in fantasy.

When I look at Buckham's pictures, I do so with the knowledge of direct experience. Through filming and presenting the BBC television series *Scotland from the Sky*, I have had the unique opportunity to fly over large parts of the country in light aircraft, in helicopters and, just like Buckham, in vintage, open-cockpit biplanes.

His images are moments of wonderful, poised stillness – his aircraft like birds, soaring effortlessly on thermals, while land and sun and sky

↑
2. *Amateur Photographer*, 25 April 1928, 27.2 × 21.1 cm. Collection of Richard and John Buckham

↗
3. *Morning Post*, 11 August 1934, 61 × 48 cm. Collection of Richard and John Buckham

put on a show all around. The reality of *actually* being in one of these aircraft is rather different. What you do not get from his works is the incessant roar of the air, the visceral assault of the wind, the sometimes brutal cold of altitude (these were all things that Buckham documented, endured, even revelled in, as he conducted his aerial adventures around Britain and then overseas, culminating in an epic flight up and down the Andean spine of South America). And yet, despite this, and despite my own experiences, it does not matter.

During filming for the television series, I took a flight one evening, during the last days of summer, in a 1949 Tiger Moth. Our route was south and west, from the aerodrome at Perth towards an airfield at Cumbernauld. There was a smattering of clouds, but the sun was low and dipping, folding golden light across a landscape that I knew very well – Perthshire is where I grew up – but had never seen before from the sky. Fields were rippling and undulating in bright greens and browns, hay-bales cast long, dark shadows, the mountains to the north-west were fringed with a reddening glow. As we continued south, the land dropped away from the Ochil Hills to the flood plain of the River Forth, and we flew right alongside the top of the tall stone tower of the National Wallace Monument. I was taking photographs as we went, and all the time I was being buffeted and pulled and pushed by the wind, the Tiger Moth rolling and dipping and fighting against the air. If I think hard about it, I can recall the acute physical discomfort, the elements of struggle, the sensual battering. But that is not how I actually remember this flight. Quite the opposite. What I picture instead is that radiant summer-evening light, that beautiful stillness, and a sense of weightless grace.

While I was preparing to write this introduction, Louise Pearson, National Galleries curator and the author of this book, showed me many of the photographs from Alfred Buckham's archive. Among them was one picture of the National Wallace Monument, with a biplane rising up against a burgeoning cloudscape (4). Light is hitting the hills, and the aircraft hangs serenely in the sky, at once fragile and majestic. Seeing it prompted a jolt of instant recognition. With that image, there is no need to describe my own flight over the same landscape any further. The noise and the wind all fall away. Buckham has stripped them back to unveil the true convergence of my own experience and memory. I can simply point to the picture and tell you: '*That* is exactly what it felt like.'

→
4. *The Wallace Monument.*
Near Stirling, *c*.1920, gelatin
silver print, 46 × 38 cm. Collection
of Richard and John Buckham

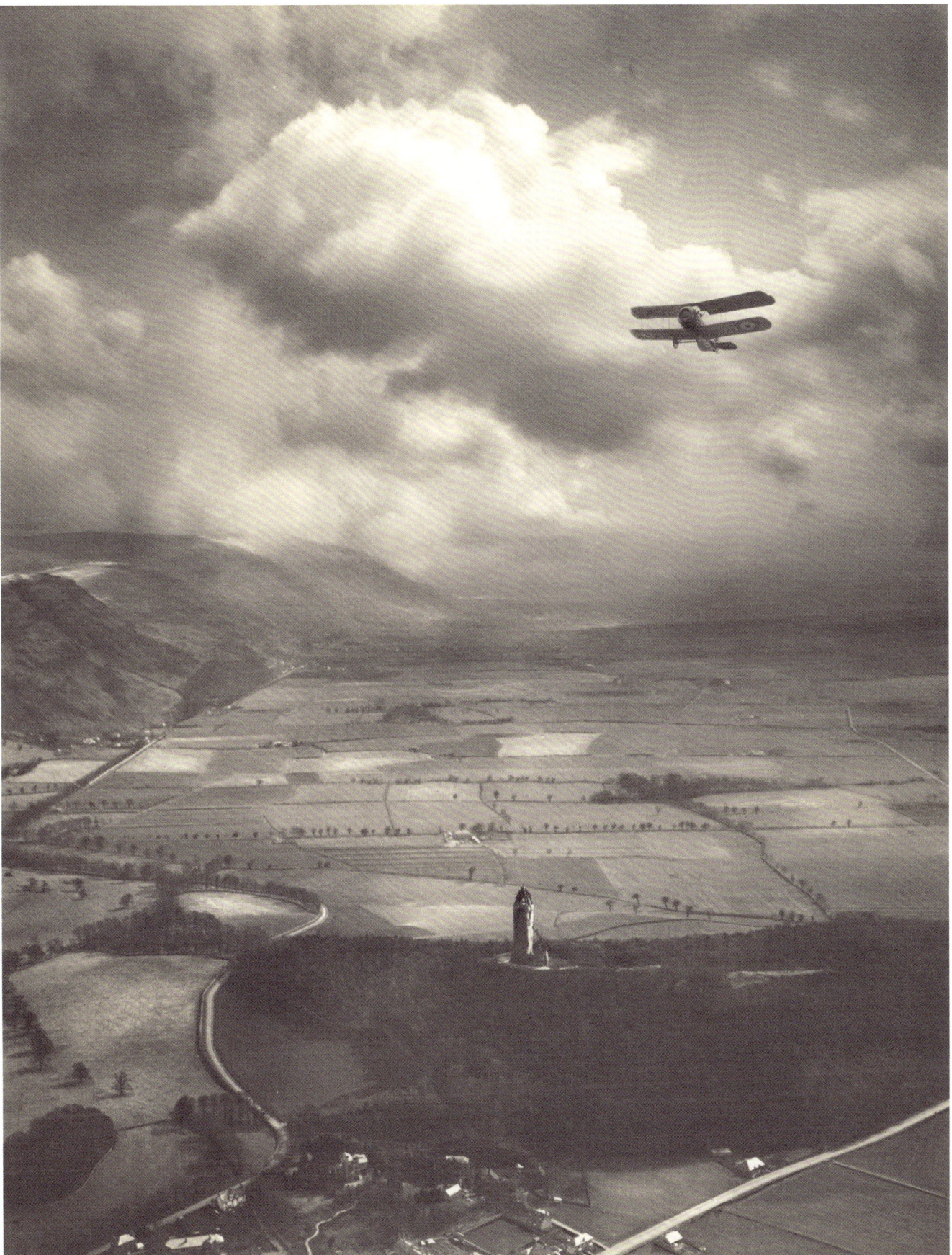

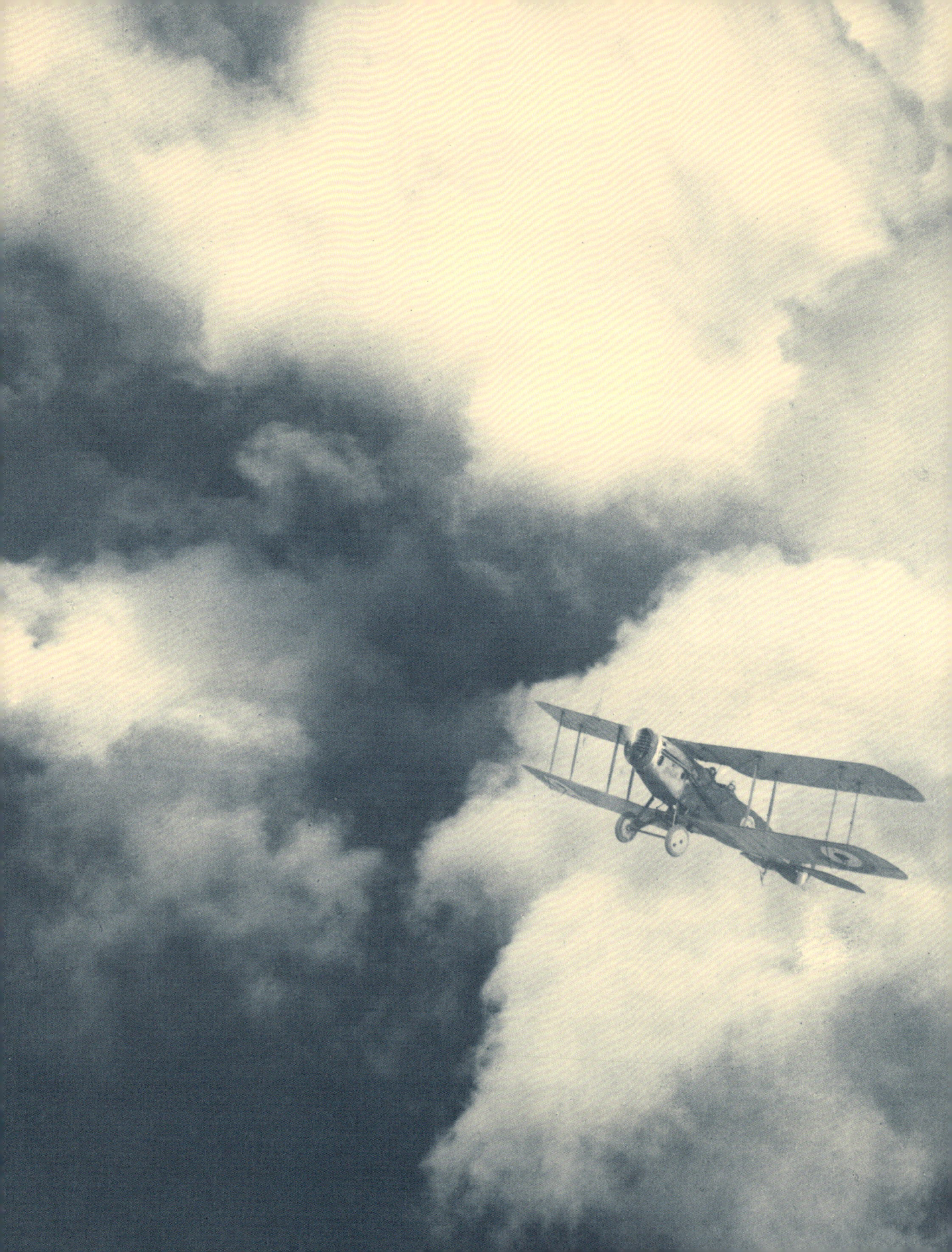

In the Air

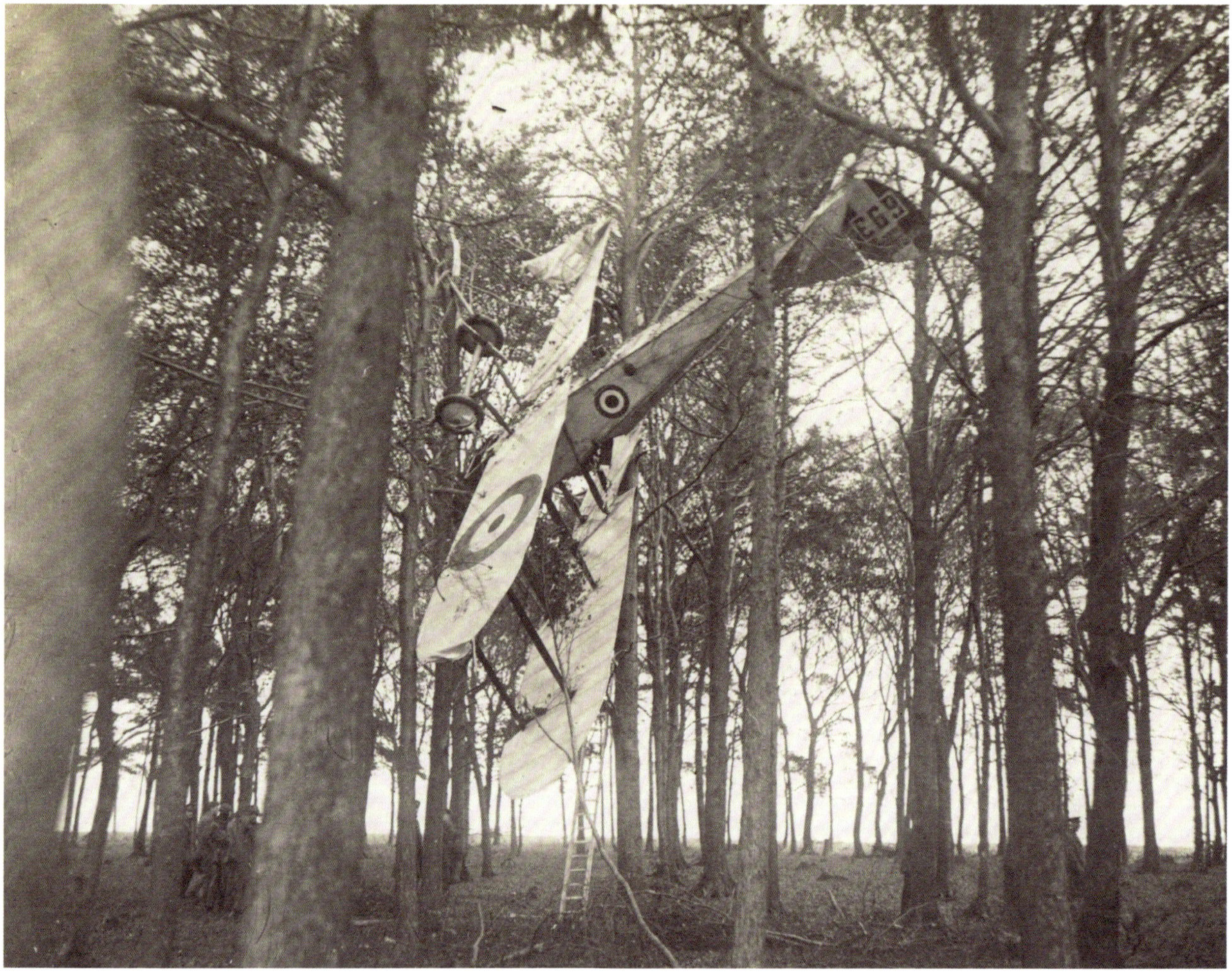

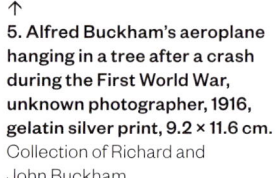

ALFRED BUCKHAM (1879–1956) was a daredevil photographer. A maverick of early aviation, he created his own unique style of photography by combining daring exploits in the air with innovation in the darkroom. The phenomenal story of his aerial photography begins in Scotland and culminates with an epic expedition across South America.

Reflecting in the *New York Times Magazine* on his various mishaps and near-misses, Buckham recalled: 'But such unpleasing circumstances are mostly forgotten, or only serve to add spice to the remembrance. Ah! One was a rare daredevil in those days!'[1]

Born in London in 1879, Buckham spent much of his early career teaching photography. He became a fellow of the Royal Photographic Society in 1913 and by the First World War was an experienced lecturer.[2] On joining the Royal Naval Air Service (a precursor to the Royal Air Force) in 1916 he was initially deployed teaching young recruits the basics of photography.[3] Requesting a transfer to active service, Buckham began his own aerial reconnaissance career based at RAF Turnhouse,

↑
5. Alfred Buckham's aeroplane hanging in a tree after a crash during the First World War, unknown photographer, 1916, gelatin silver print, 9.2 × 11.6 cm. Collection of Richard and John Buckham

→
6. Alfred Buckham wearing goggles, unknown photographer, c.1918, gelatin silver print, 29.5 × 20.5 cm. Collection of Richard and John Buckham

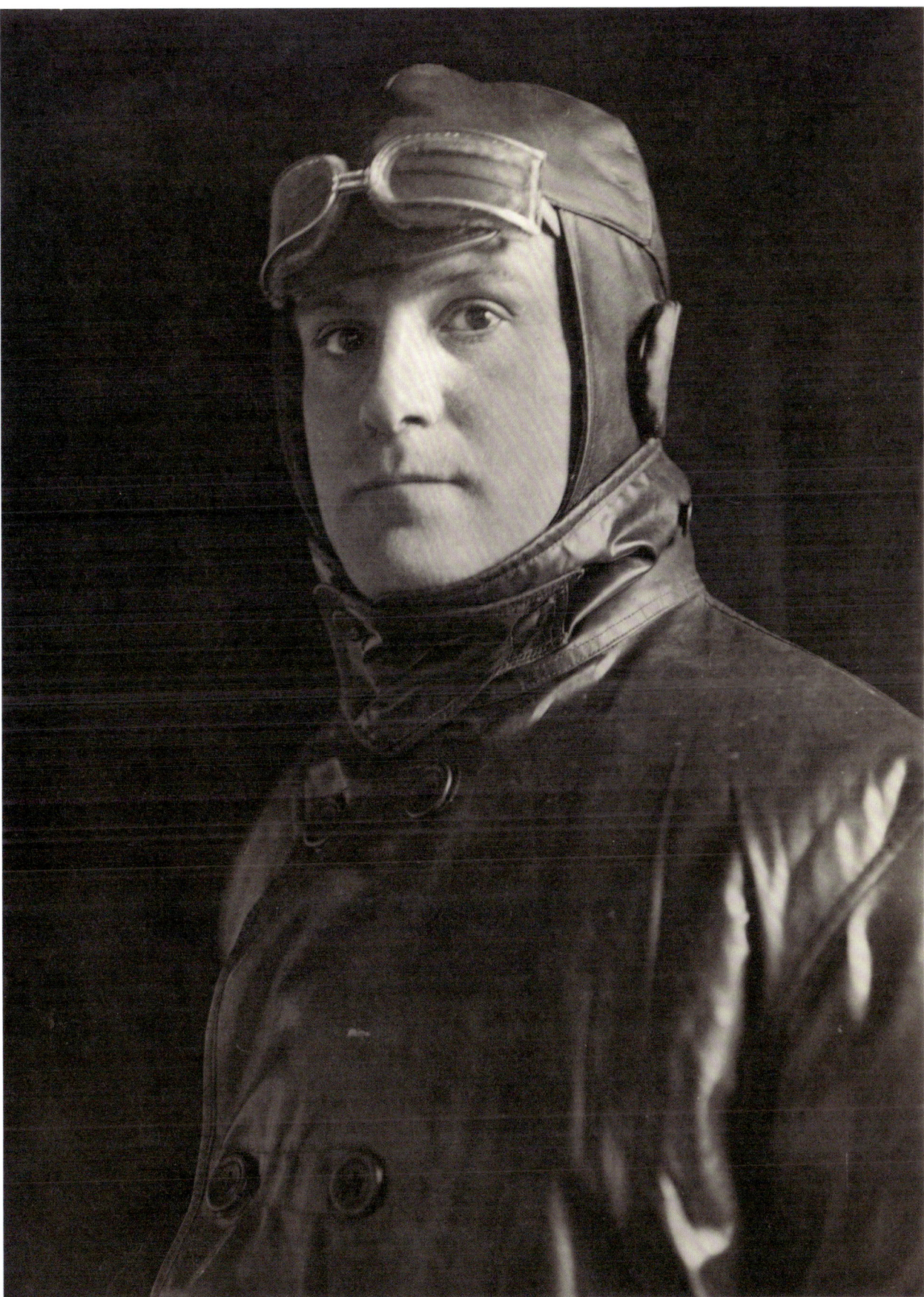

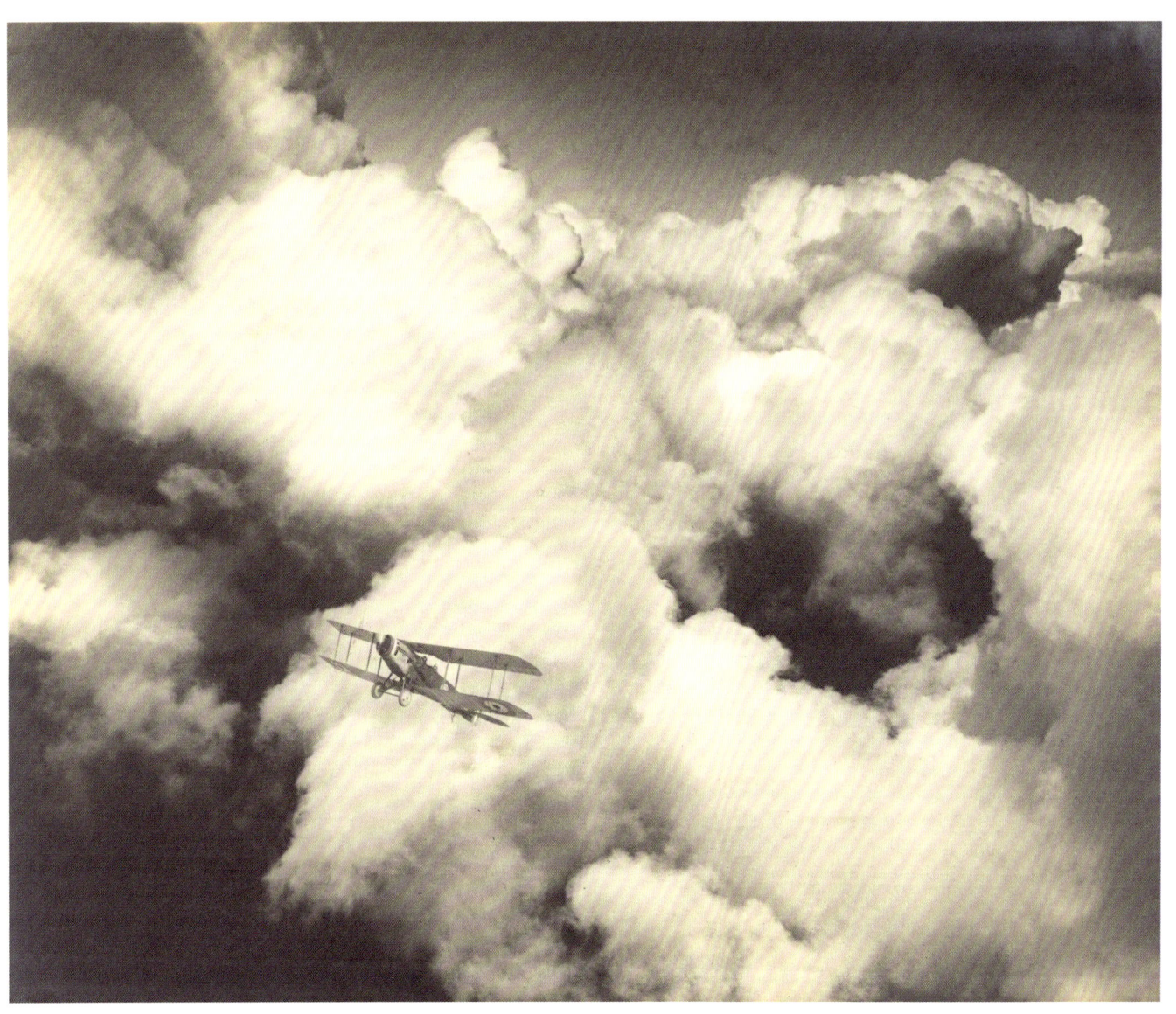

↑
7. Bristol Fighter in Flight,
*c.*1920, gelatin silver print,
37.7 × 45.7 cm. Collection of
Richard and John Buckham

→
8. Sunshine, and Snow
Showers, *c.*1920, gelatin silver
print, 45.5 × 37.7 cm. National
Galleries of Scotland. Purchased
with Art Fund support, 2008

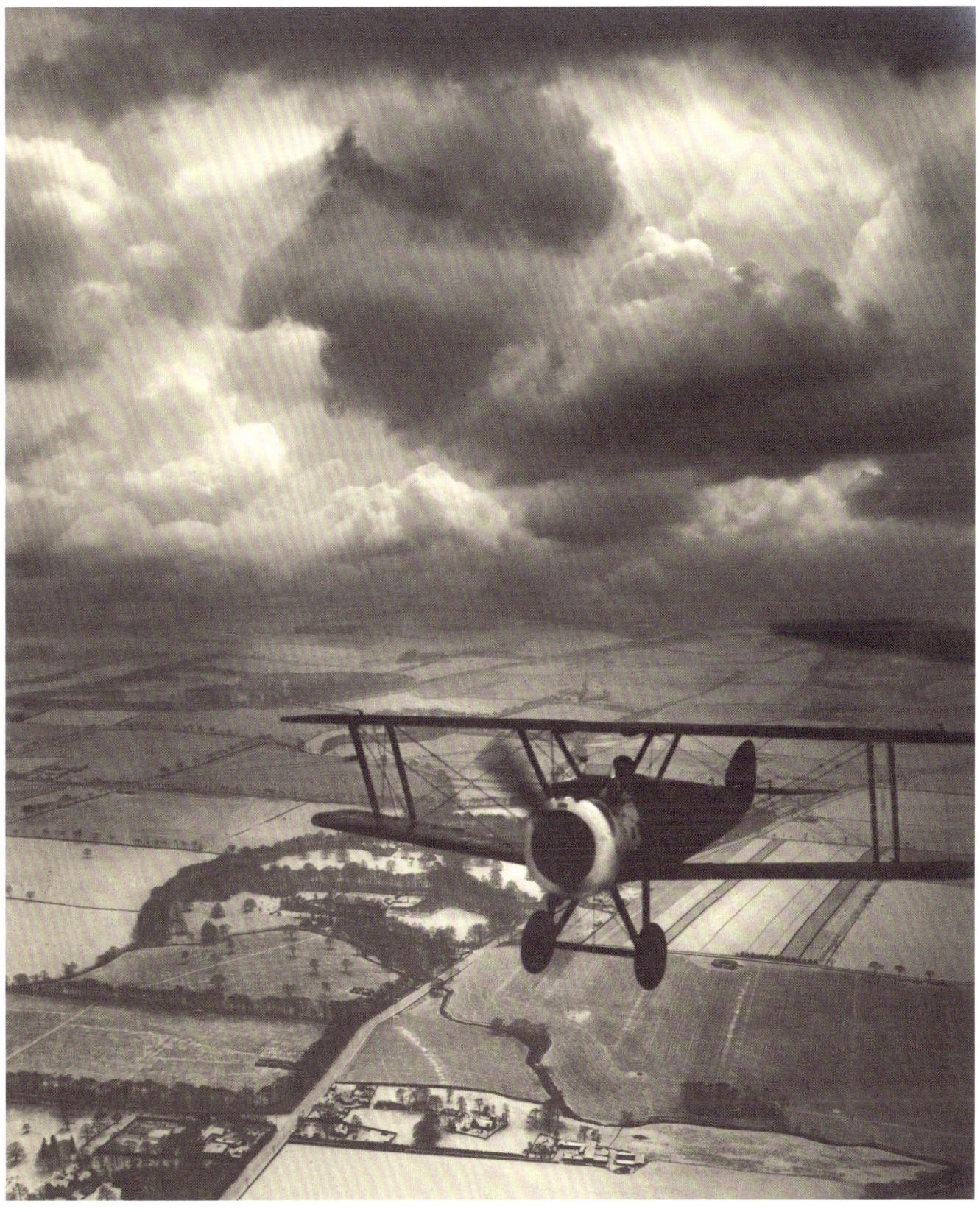

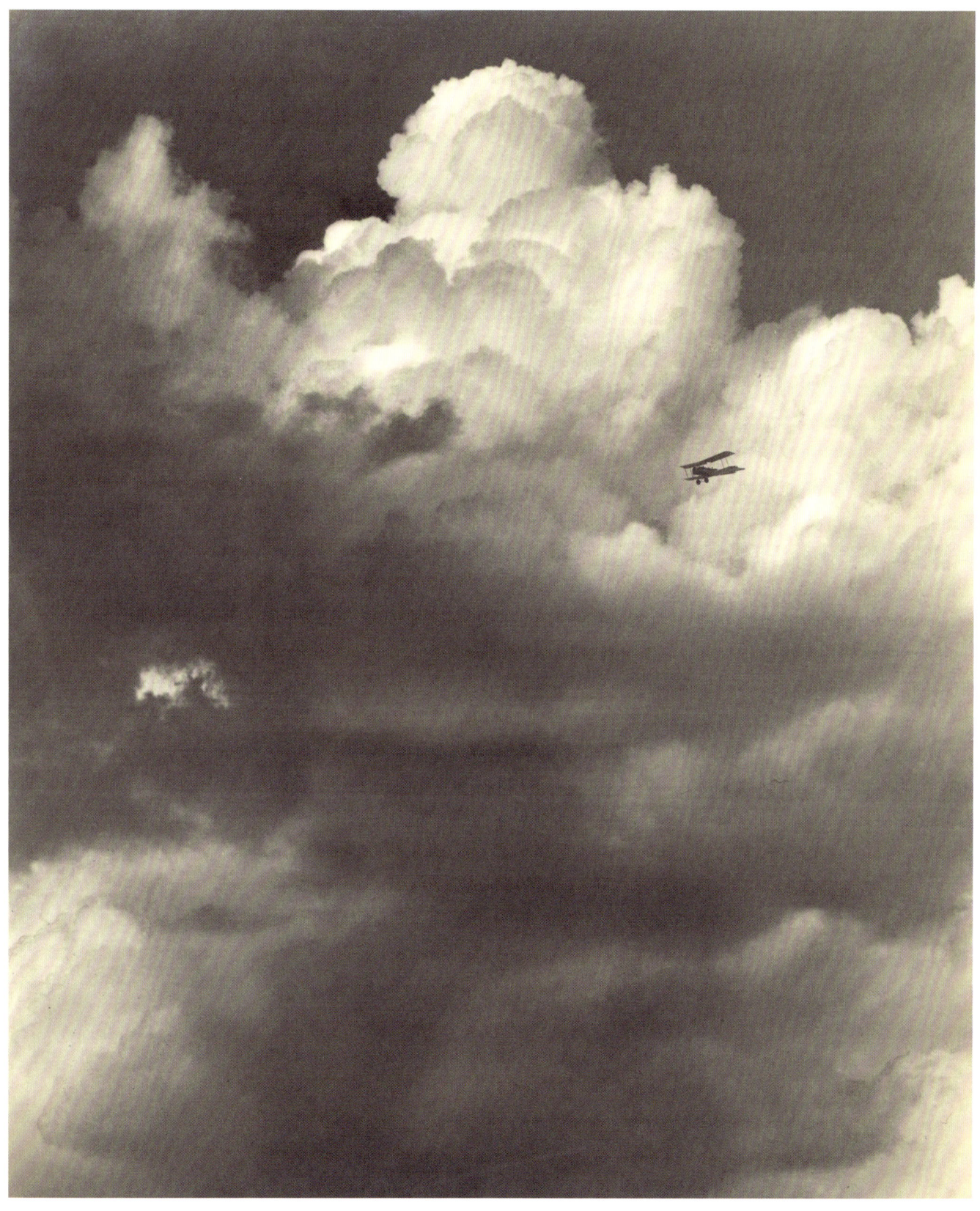

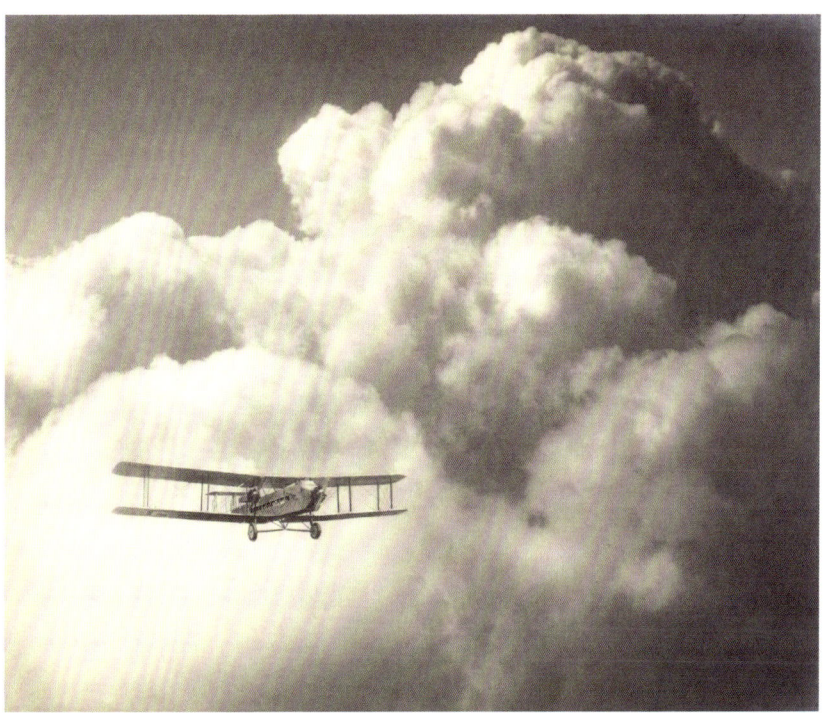

9. *Where Lightnings Lurk*,
*c.*1920, gelatin silver print,
45.1 × 37.8 cm. Collection of
Richard and John Buckham

10. *Argosy in Flight*, *c.*1928,
gelatin silver print, 37.5 × 45.8 cm.
Collection of Richard and
John Buckham

now Edinburgh Airport. His military records testify that he had an
'exceptional' talent for flying, and he was promoted to captain within a
year.[4] It was an extremely dangerous occupation, with life expectancy
measured in days not years.

During his military career, Buckham crashed a terrifying nine times.[5]
He emerged relatively unscathed from the first eight of these, some of
which are documented in his wartime scrapbooks. One image, captioned
'10 Oct. 1916 I again crash in woods. Edwards killed 2 days later', shows
the wreak of an aeroplane hanging precariously from the branch of a
tree (5). His descriptions of these crashes are vivid: 'When I discovered
myself again, I was head foremost in a particularly wicked bush, which
was doing its best to indicate the intrusion was unwelcomed. But when
I endeavoured to extricate myself it became positively cantankerous;
and what I called that bush none but myself will ever know.'[6]

The ninth crash, over Rosyth, was serious. He suffered a throat injury
leading to the removal of his larynx.[7] For the rest of his life, he relied
on a tube inserted in his neck to breathe and could only raise his voice
to a whisper. In 1919 he was assessed as fully disabled and discharged
from military service on a full pension.[8] It is quite remarkable then that
Buckham retained his appetite for flying and continued to pursue aerial
photography after the war.

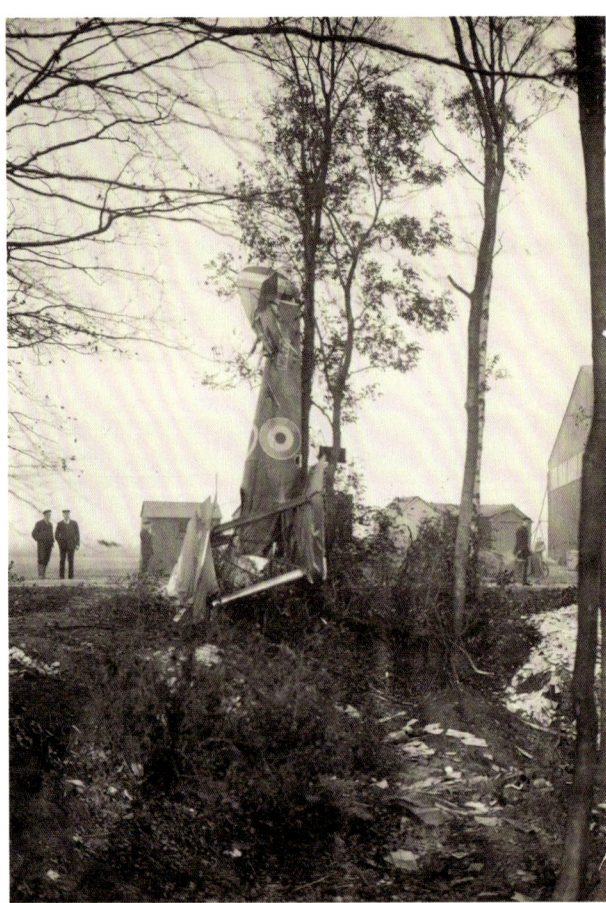

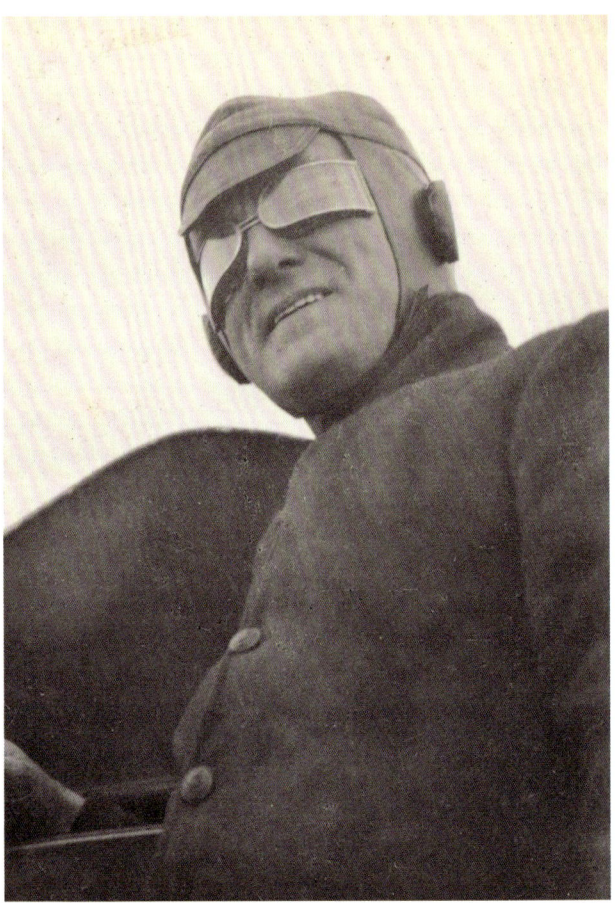

Despite the obvious danger, Buckham's approach to flying appears to have been characterised by a rather relaxed approach to safety:

Providing the pilot knows what one is doing, it is quite unnecessary to wear a safety belt which badly impedes movement; and the man with the joy-stick can always be relied upon to pass the word if he contemplates banking or diving the machine. It is not easy to tumble out of an aeroplane, unless you really want to, and on considerably more than a thousand flights I have used a safety belt only once, and then it was thrust upon me. I always stand up to make an exposure and, taking the precaution to tie my right leg to the seat, I am free to move rapidly, and easily, in any desired direction; and loop the loop; and indulge in other such delights, with perfect safety.[9]

To capture the clearest aerial photographs, he favoured 'the open cockpit of a not-too-speedy airplane'.[10] This was crucial as the faster the aeroplane, the harder it became to secure a sharp image. In an article for *Camera Craft* he noted that: 'Unfortunately for the budding aerial photographer the work becomes less easy of accomplishment year by year owing to the stupid craze for "saving time" which demands faster and still faster machines.'[11]

↖
11. Plane crash during the First World War, unknown photographer, *c*.1918, gelatin silver print, 15 × 10.5 cm. Collection of Richard and John Buckham

↑
12. Alfred Buckham in flying clothes, unknown photographer, *c*.1918, gelatin silver print, 8.5 × 6.8 cm. Collection of Richard and John Buckham

→
13. *The Loop, *c*.1920, gelatin silver print, 45.5 × 27.5 cm. National Galleries of Scotland. Purchased in recognition of over 40 years of work on the National Galleries of Scotland photography collection by James Berry, Senior Paper Conservator

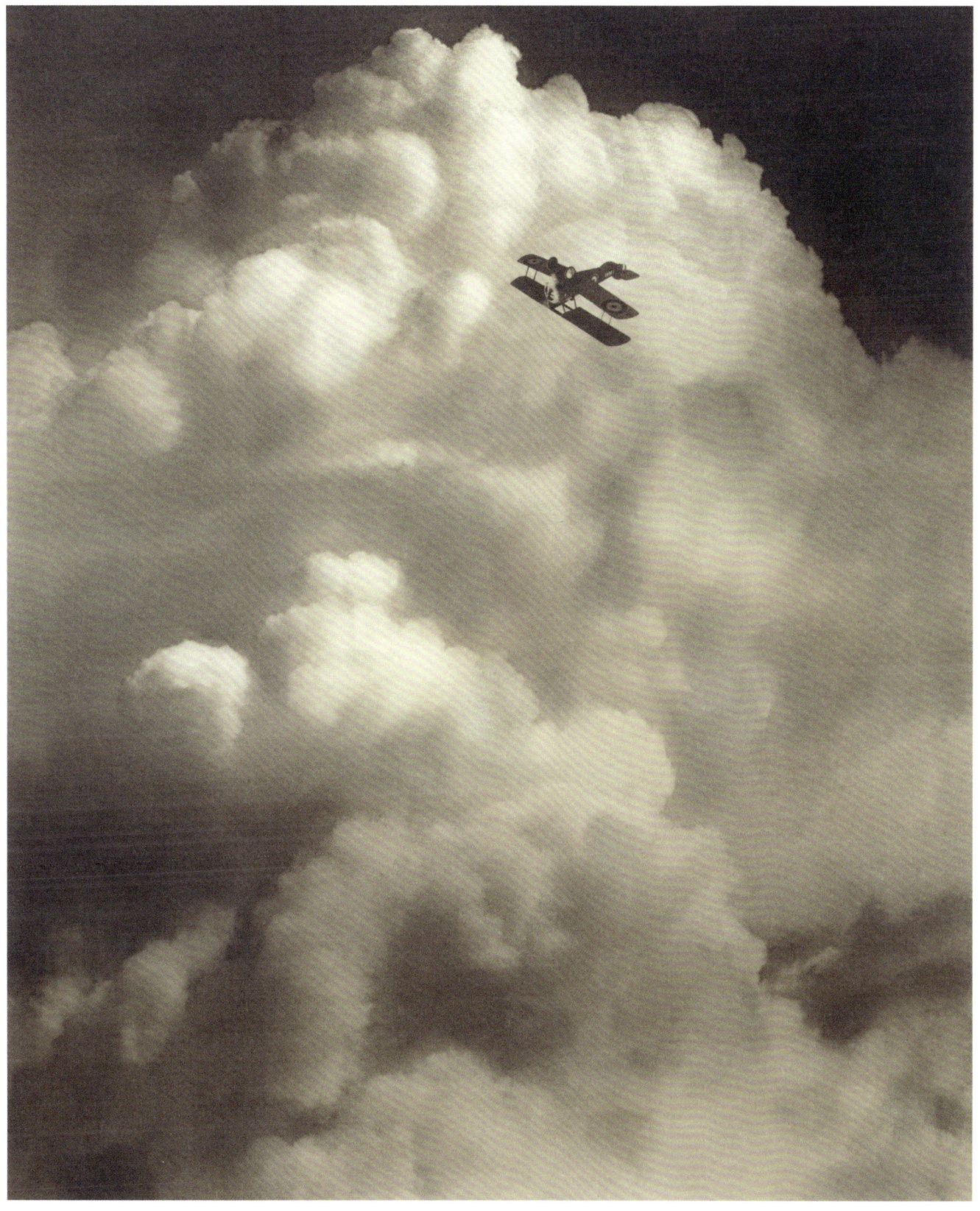

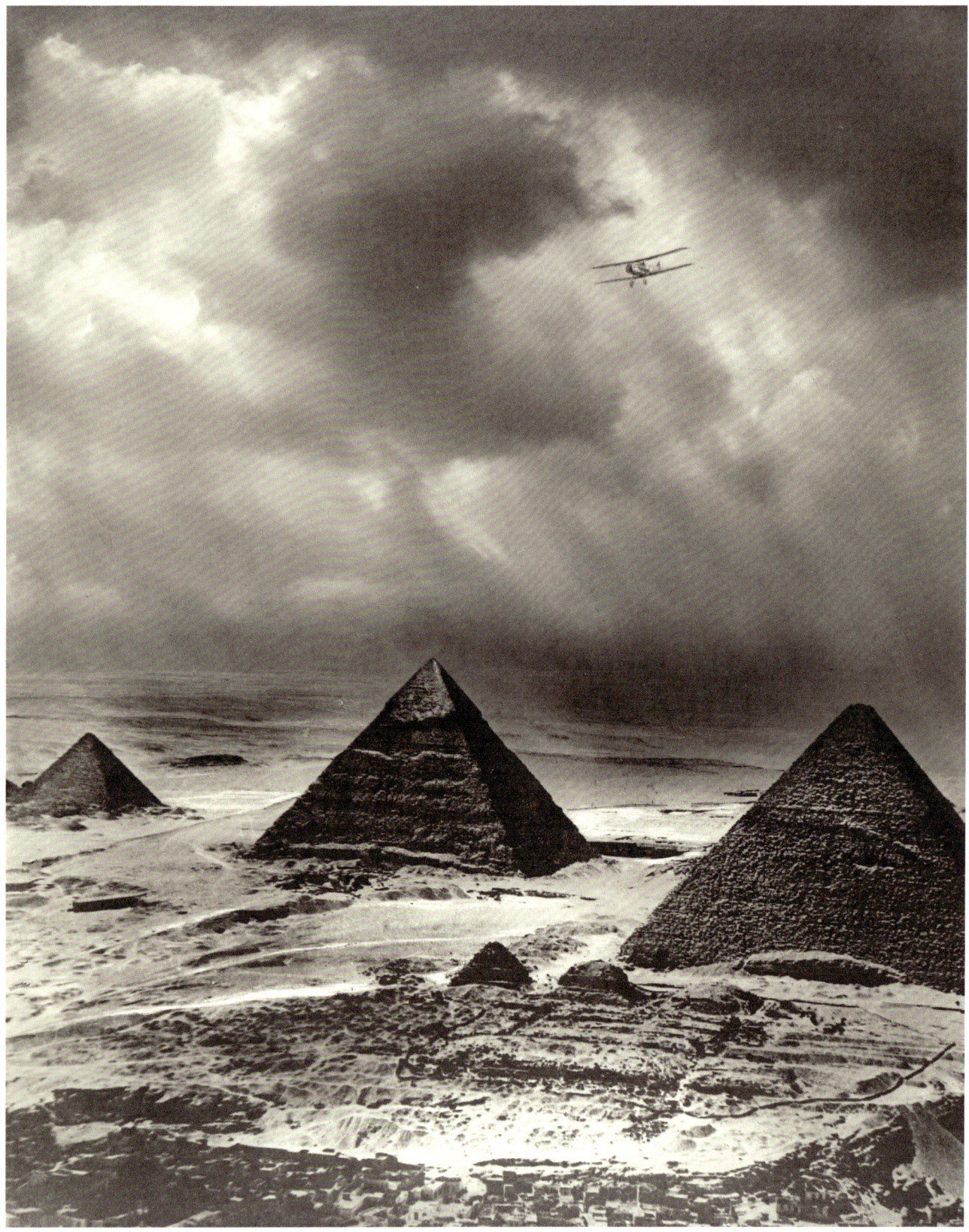

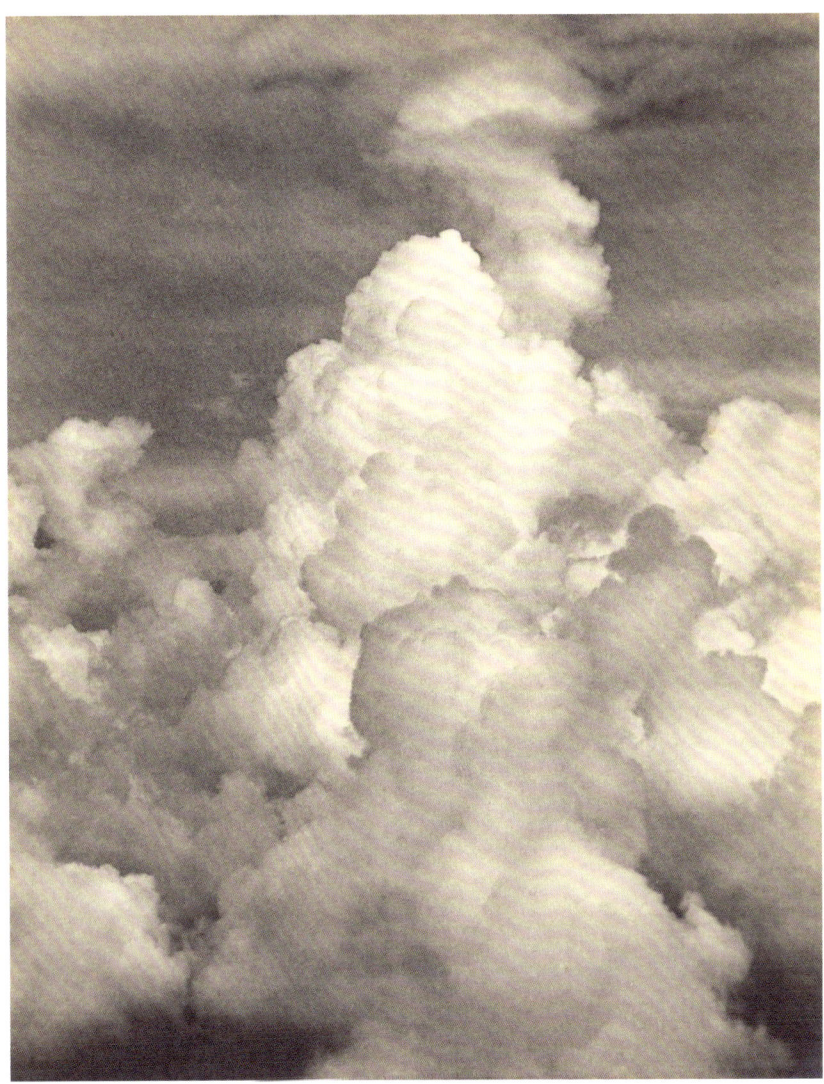

He was also adamant that it was essential to stand up to make an exposure. Otherwise, the negative would be spoiled by the vibrations of the aeroplane as the camera would inevitably come into contact with the side of the cockpit.[12] He did concede, however, that 'it is an alarming experience for a beginner to find himself lolling over the side of an aeroplane while the landscape climbs up to the sky, and the horizon loses its horizontality and endeavours to become vertical'.[13]

Buckham's photographs record the aircraft taking to the skies in the early days of aviation. This included the aeroplanes he was familiar with such as the Bristol Fighter, a two-seat biplane designed for aerial reconnaissance (7). He also photographed the R-100 (17) and R-101 (16), bizarre examples of rigid airships that the British government hoped would transform passenger air travel in the 1920s. It was an exciting

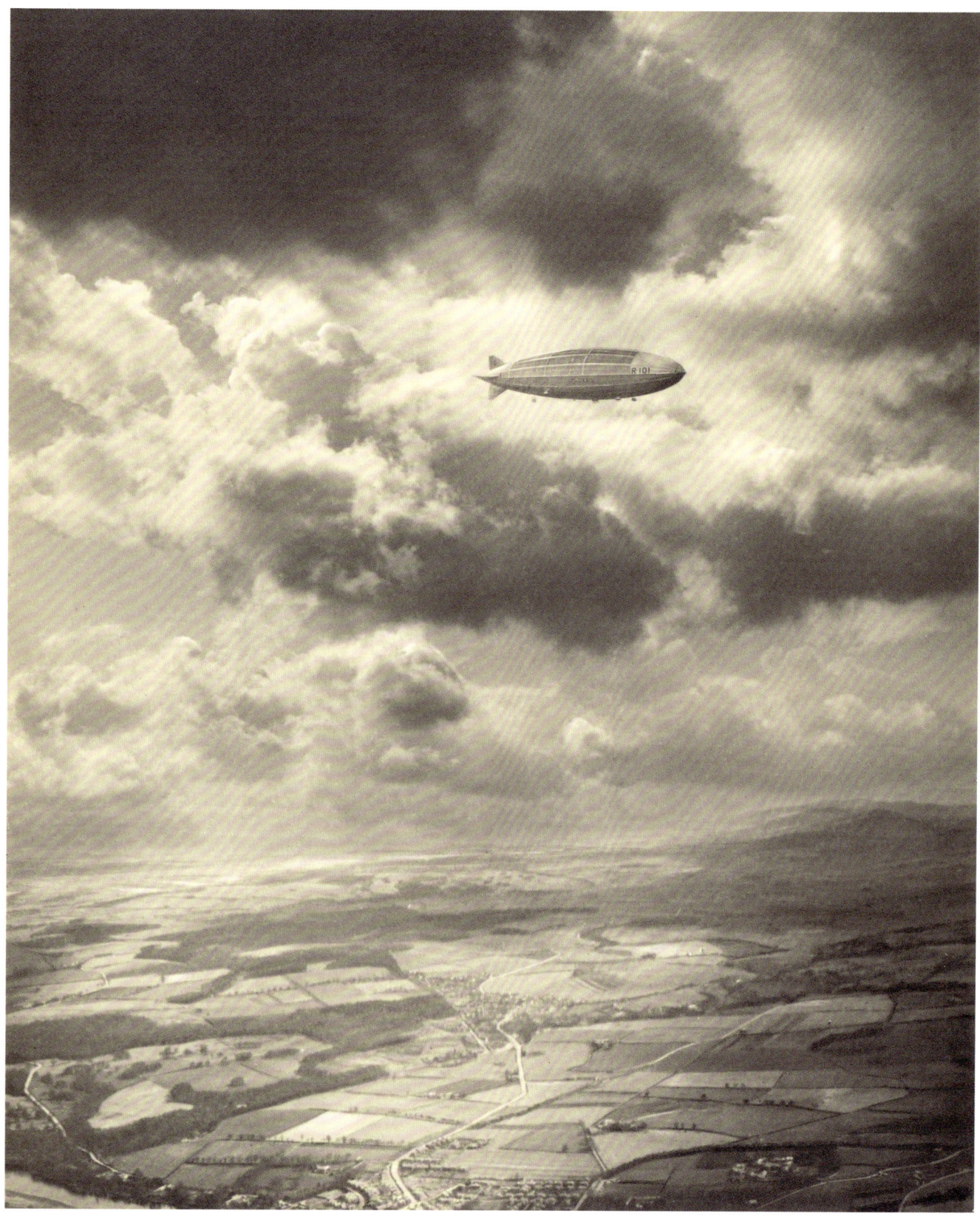

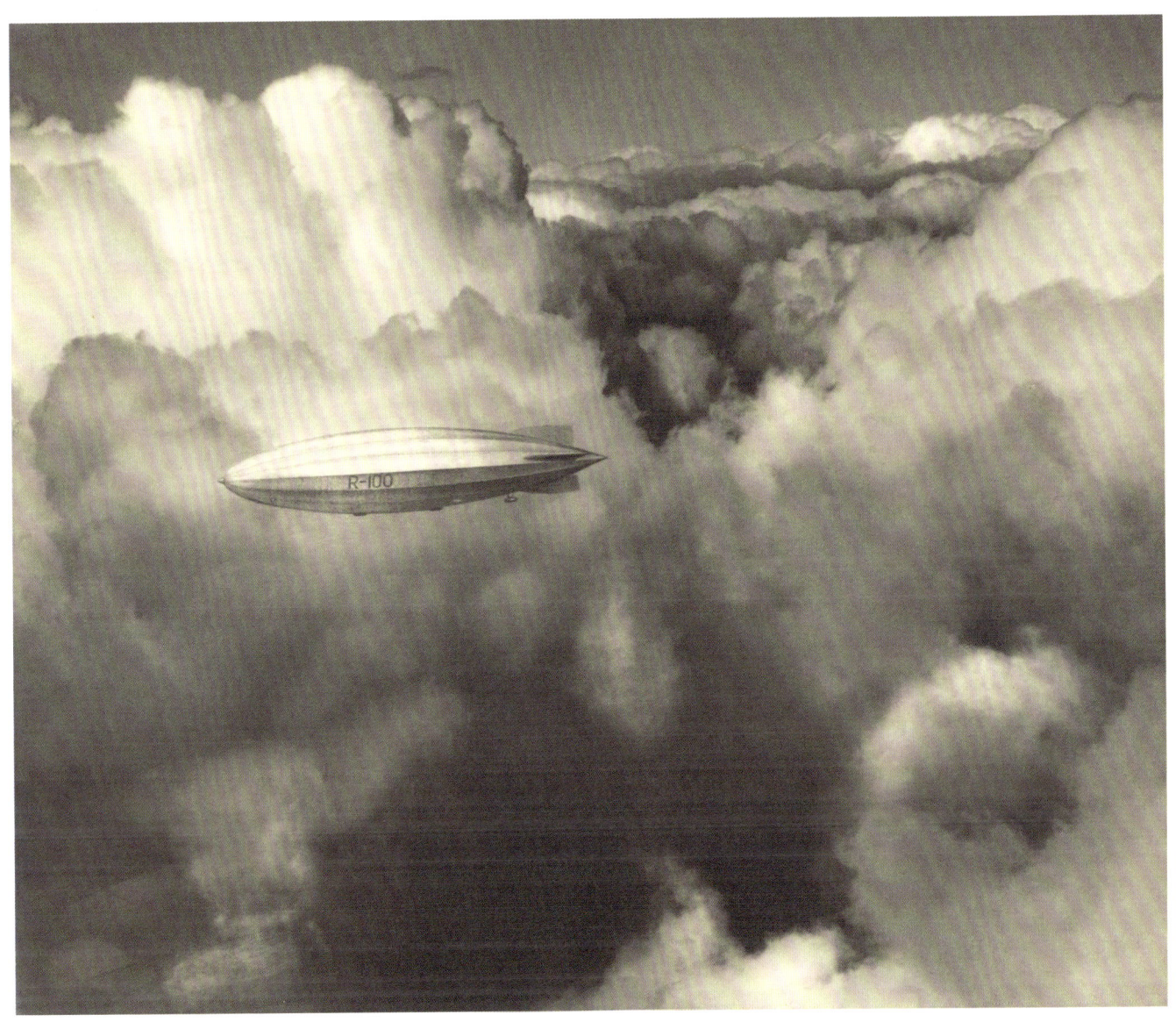

16. *R-101*, *c*.1930, gelatin silver print, 45.6 × 38.1 cm. Collection of Richard and John Buckham

17. *R-100*, *c*.1930, gelatin silver print, 38.5 × 46 cm. National Galleries of Scotland. Purchased with Art Fund support, 2008

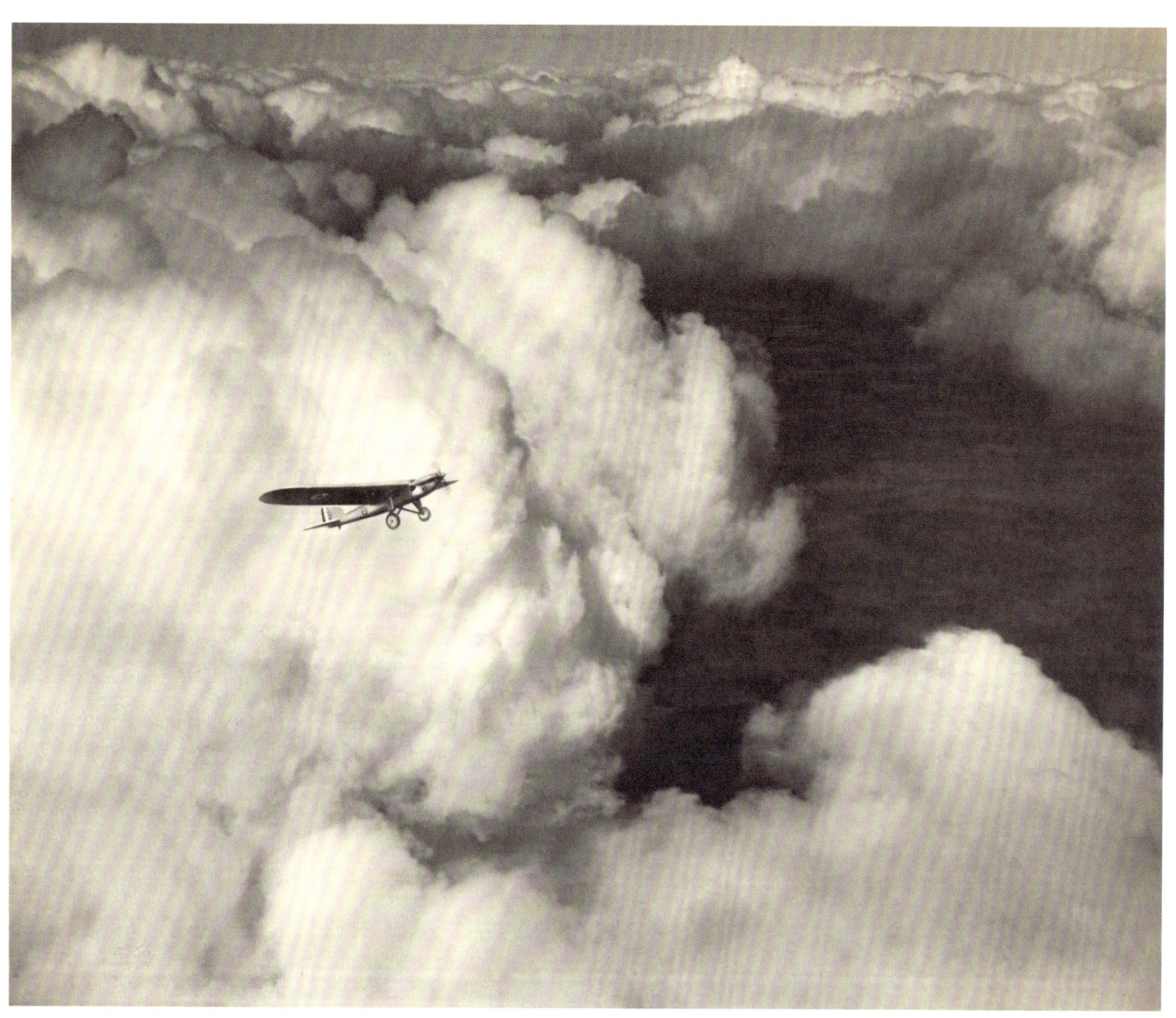

↑
18. *Fairey Napier in Flight*,
*c.*1930, gelatin silver print,
38 × 45.7 cm. Collection of
Richard and John Buckham

→
19. *Over the Alps*, *c.*1920, gelatin
silver print, 39.8 × 31.8 cm.
Collection of Richard and
John Buckham

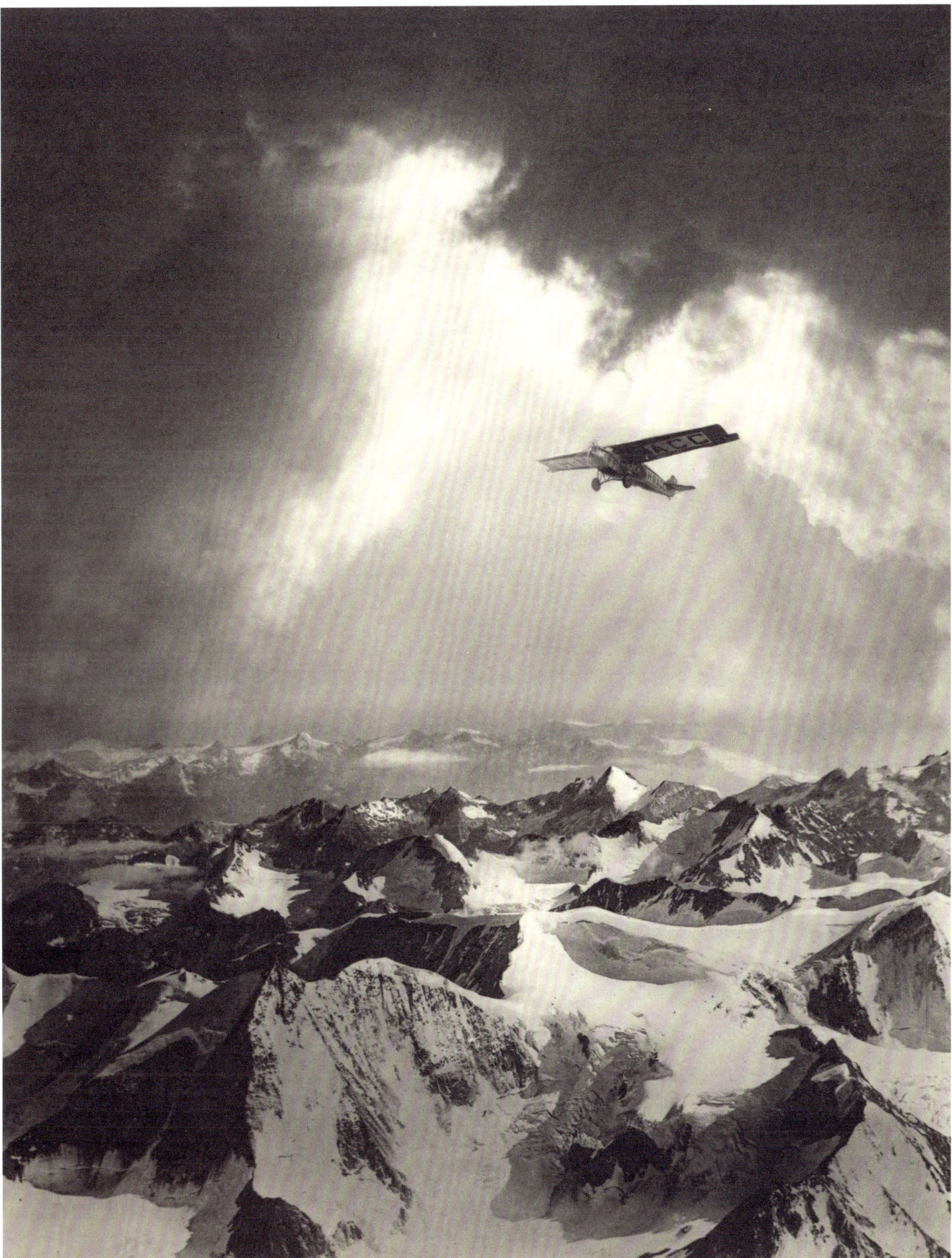

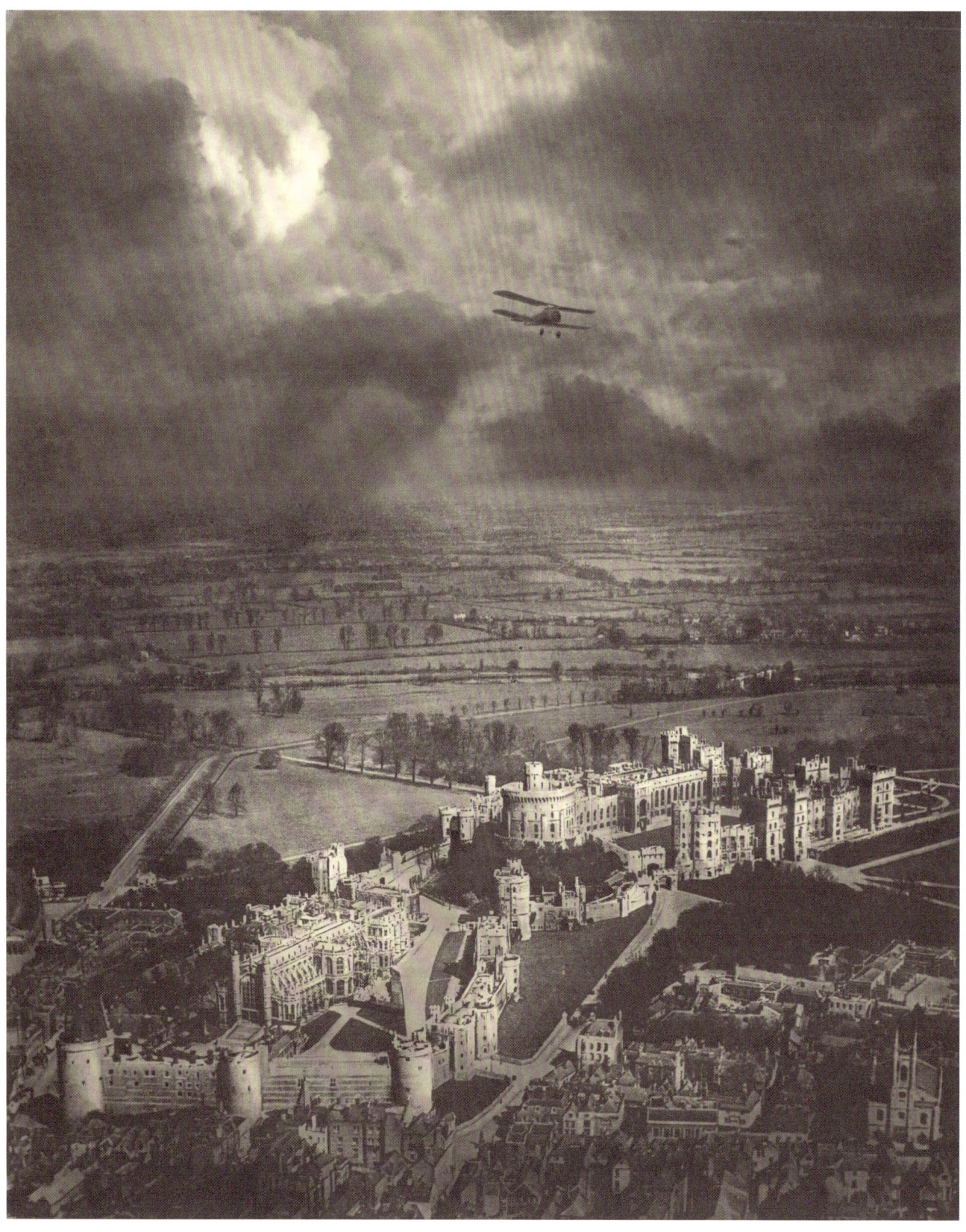

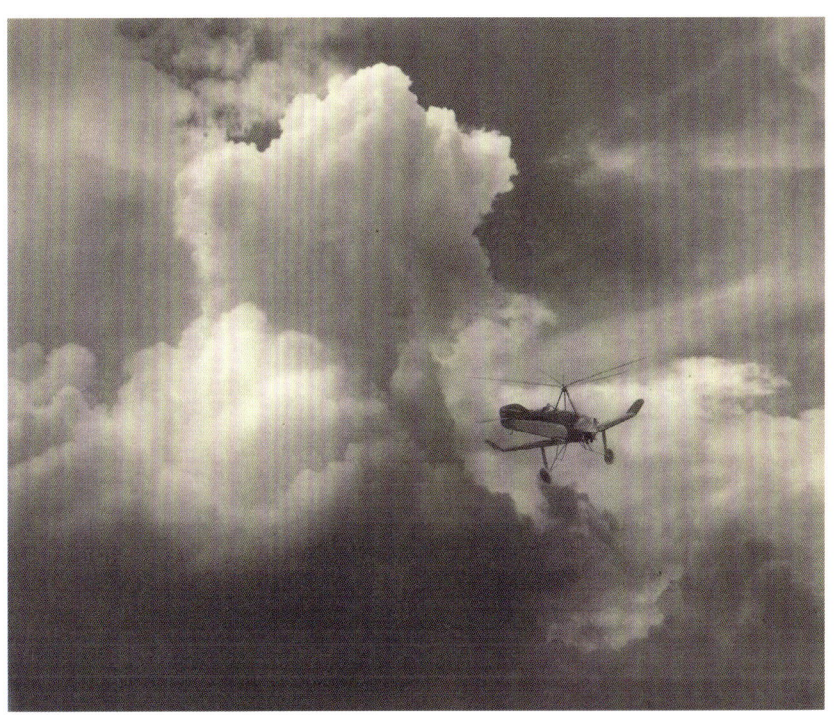

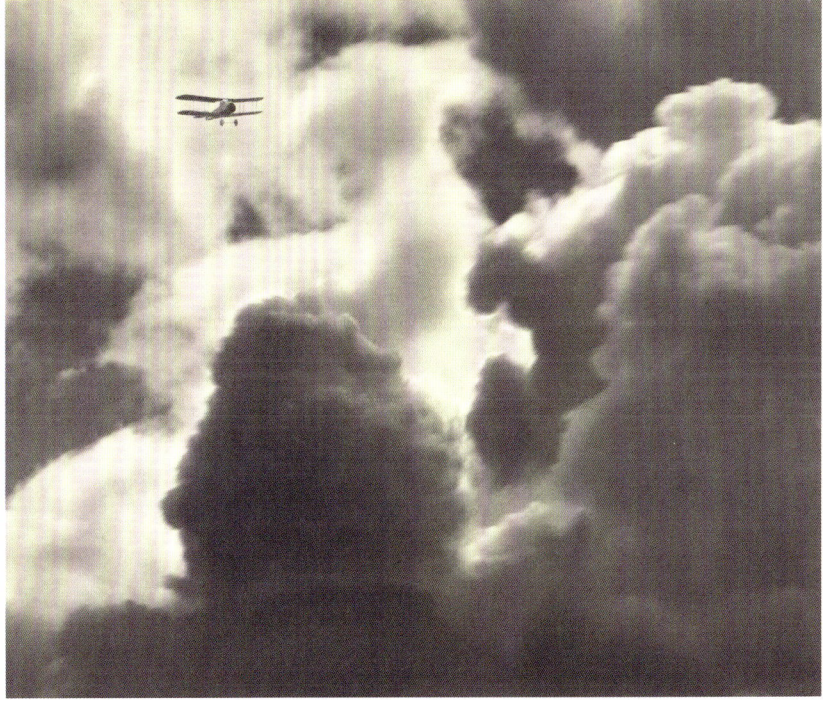

20. *Windsor Castle*, *c.*1920, gelatin
silver print, 46 × 37.9 cm. Collection
of Richard and John Buckham

21. *Autogyro*, *c.*1930, gelatin silver
print, 38.1 × 46.1 cm. National
Galleries of Scotland. Purchased
with Art Fund support, 2008

22. *The Thunderstorm*, *c.*1920,
gelatin silver print, 38.1 × 46 cm.
National Galleries of Scotland.
Purchased with Art Fund support, 2008

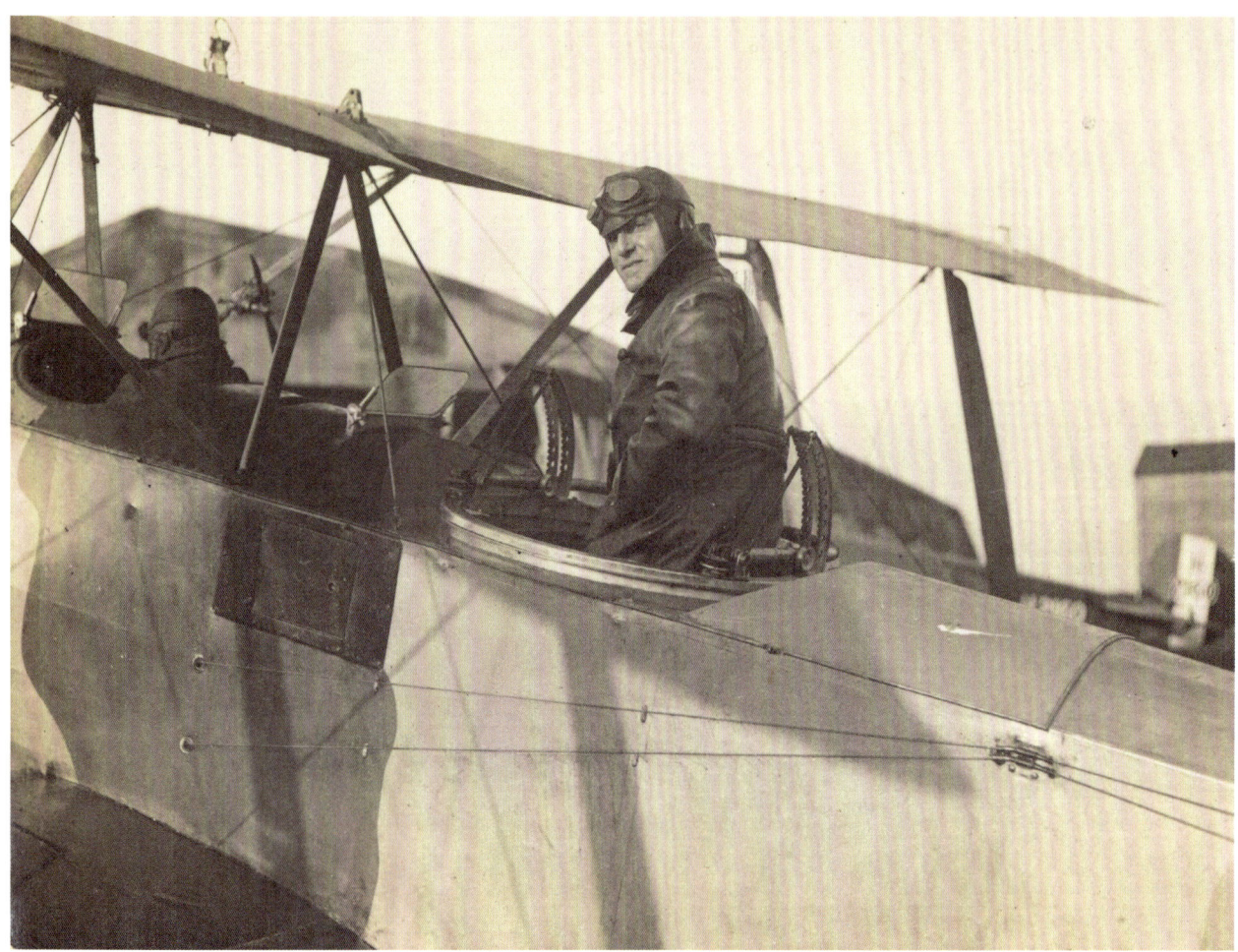

time for aviation, and Buckham aspired to recreate the feeling of flying alongside these pioneering aircraft.

Buckham was fascinated by different weather conditions. He relished the thrill of being in the heart of a storm and feeling the full force of the elements. He also believed that 'stormy days, with bursts of sunshine, and occasional showers of rain, provide the most opportunities for picturemaking', though he did warn that 'some of the effects to be seen are so exquisitely beautiful that, lost in admiration and wonder, one almost forgets to use the camera'.[14]

Many of his photographs, particularly those made in more dramatic weather conditions, have a note on the reverse recording the atmospheric conditions and the altitude at which the picture was made. For example, *The Thunderstorm* (22) was taken 'flying through a thunderstorm at 10,000 ft. The lightning was blinding and the thunder unbearably loud. The aeroplane sometimes fell several hundreds of feet in deep air pockets. Immediately after taking this photograph our machine seemed to be on fire and the pilot and myself experienced an electric shock.'

↑
23. Alfred Buckham in an aeroplane, unknown photographer, *c*.1918, gelatin silver print, 8.5 × 11.4 cm. Collection of Richard and John Buckham

→
24. *Lincoln, c.*1930, gelatin silver print, 45.5 × 38.2 cm. Collection of Richard and John Buckham

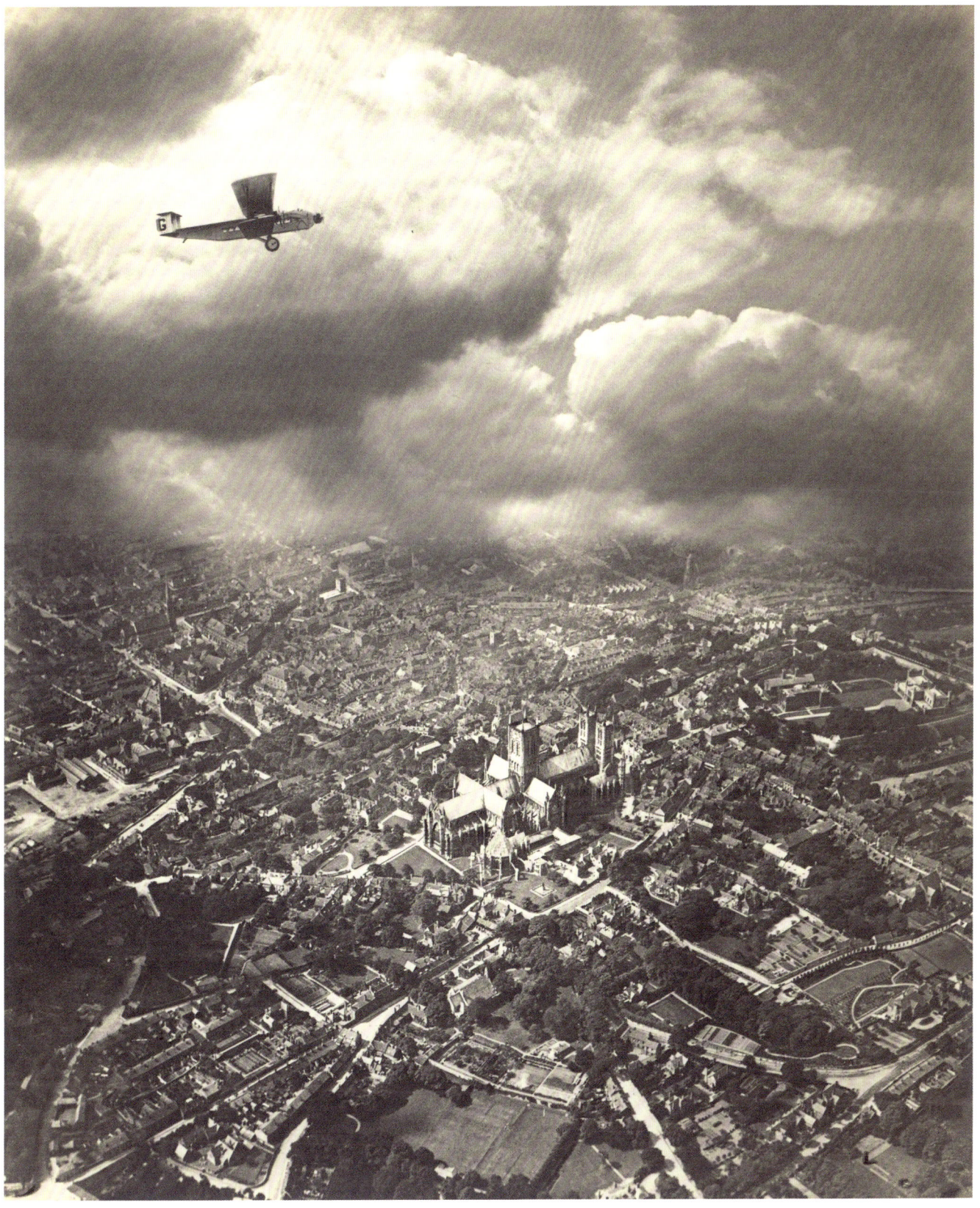

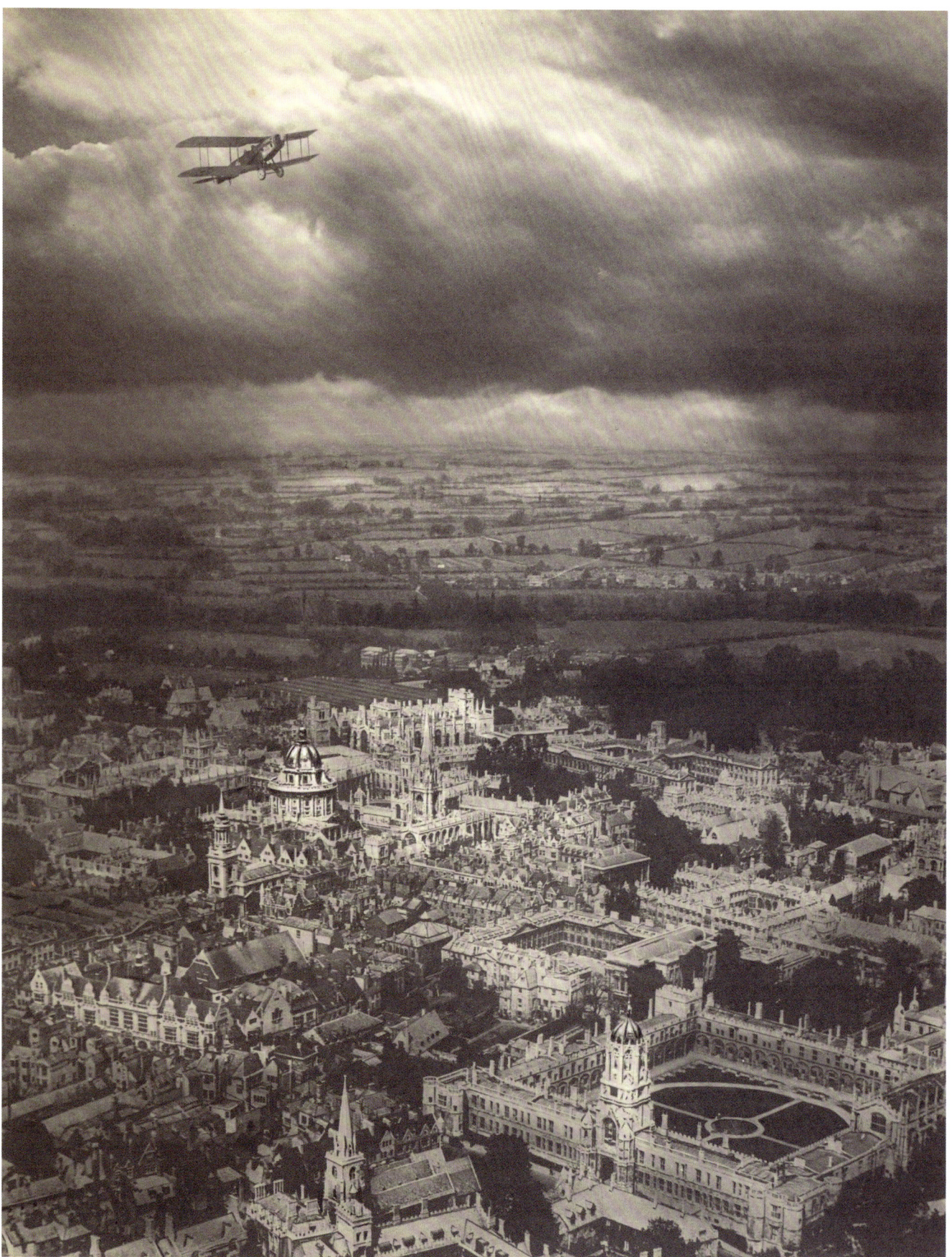

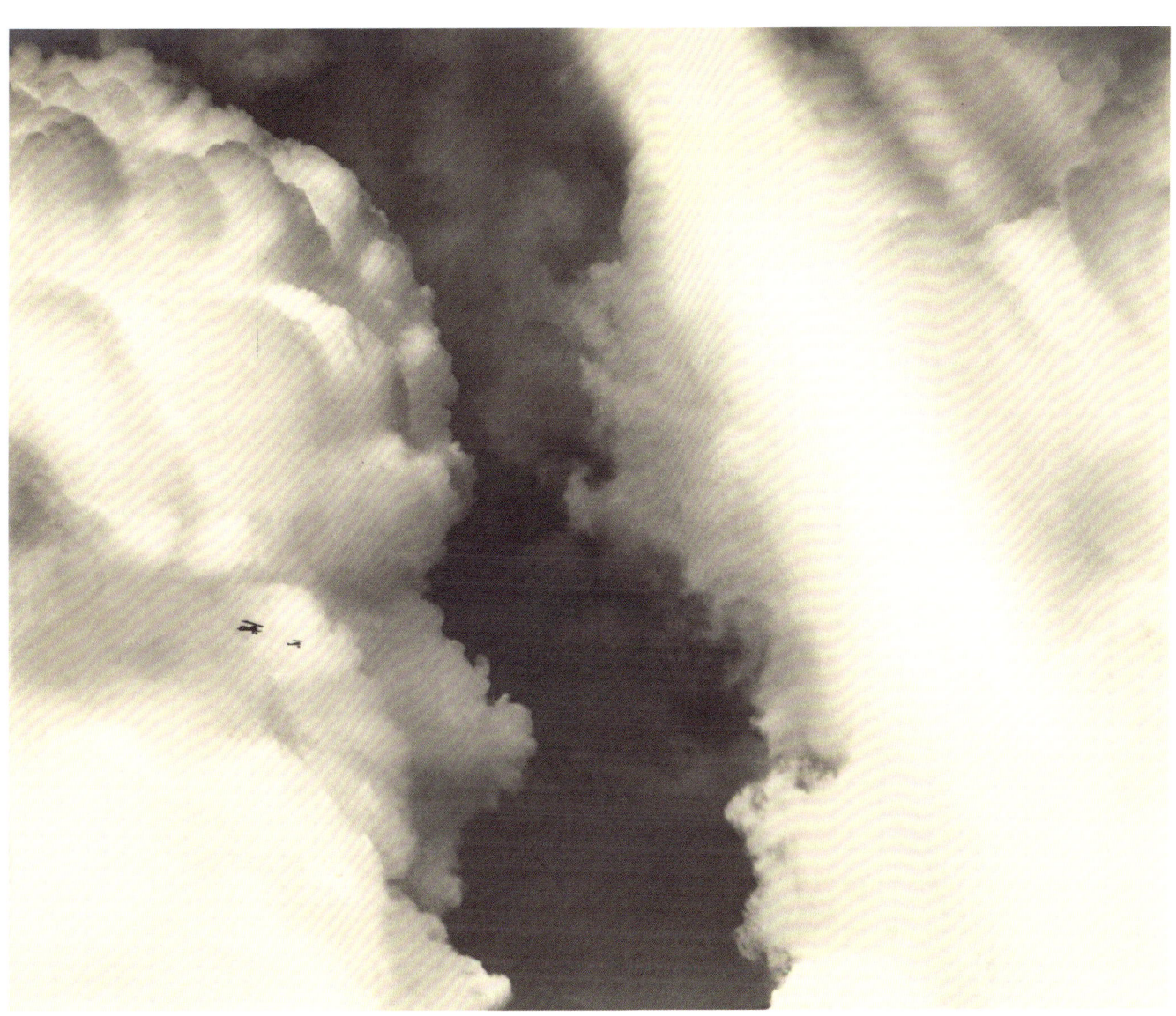

←
25. *Oxford*, *c.*1920, gelatin silver print, 46 × 37.6 cm. Collection of Richard and John Buckham

↑
26. *The Rainbow*, *c.*1920, gelatin silver print, 38.2 × 46.1 cm. National Galleries of Scotland. Purchased with Art Fund support, 2008

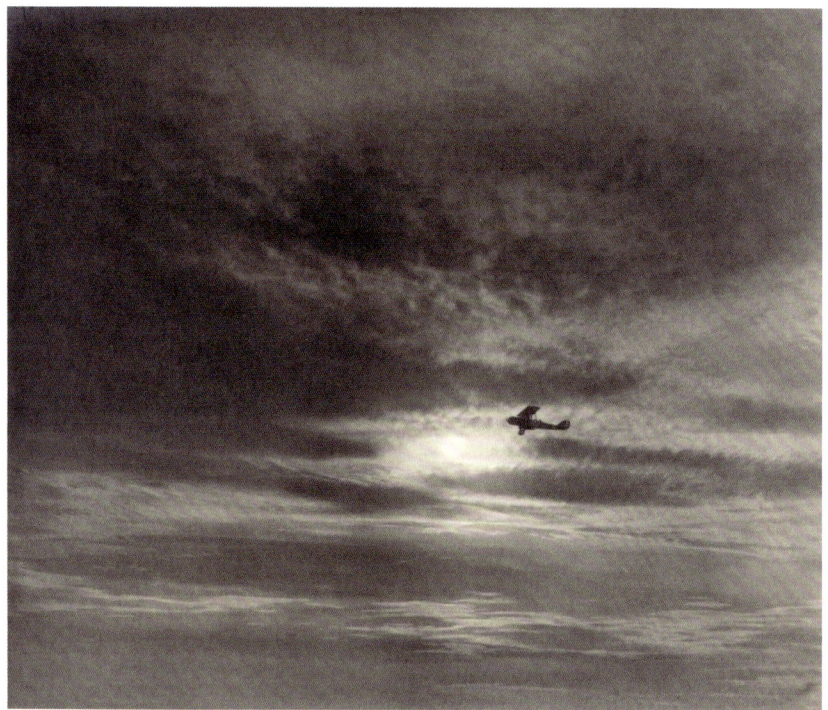

Buckham's desire to capture the awe of nature's elements can be traced back to an early interest in art and his admiration of J.M.W. Turner. As a young man he had hoped to become a painter but, discouraged after studying Turner's paintings in the National Gallery in London, he rather theatrically made a bonfire of his sketches.[15] To match the drama of his photographs, Buckham gave many of them poetic titles. Among the most whimsical is *Where Lightnings Lurk* (9).

His time in the military instilled a sense of adventure. Although based in Scotland, he made some expeditions further afield. He flew over the Alps (19) and photographed a sandstorm over the Great Pyramid of Giza in Egypt (14). These early aerial adventures provided an excellent training ground for the journey he would later make across South America, soaring over the Andes and peering into the remains of ancient civilisations buried deep within dense jungles.

Buckham also documented several English cities from the air, including London, Durham and Oxford. The most captivating of this group of urban images is *The Heart of the Empire* (28), which shows a biplane following the River Thames as it snakes through London. Now one of his most celebrated photographs, *The Heart of the Empire* was exhibited by Buckham in 1925 at the Royal Photographic Society's seventieth annual exhibition, securing his position as Britain's premier aerial photographer.[16]

↖
27. *Sunset*, *c.*1920, gelatin silver print, 38.3 × 45.7 cm. Collection of Richard and John Buckham

→
28. *The Heart of the Empire*, 1923, Bromide print, 45.6 × 37.7 cm. The Royal Photographic Society Collection at the V&A, acquired with the generous assistance of the National Lottery Heritage Fund and Art Fund

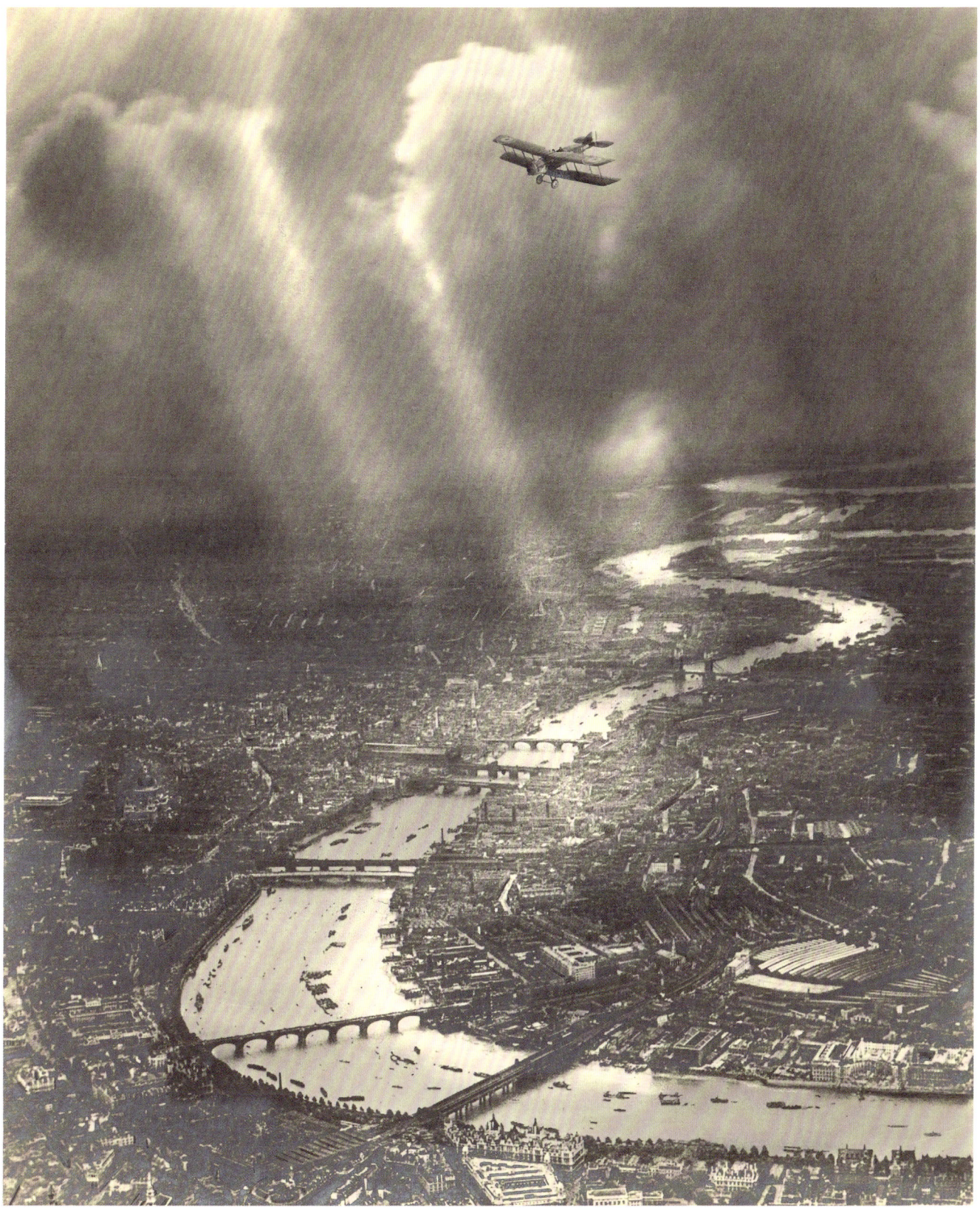

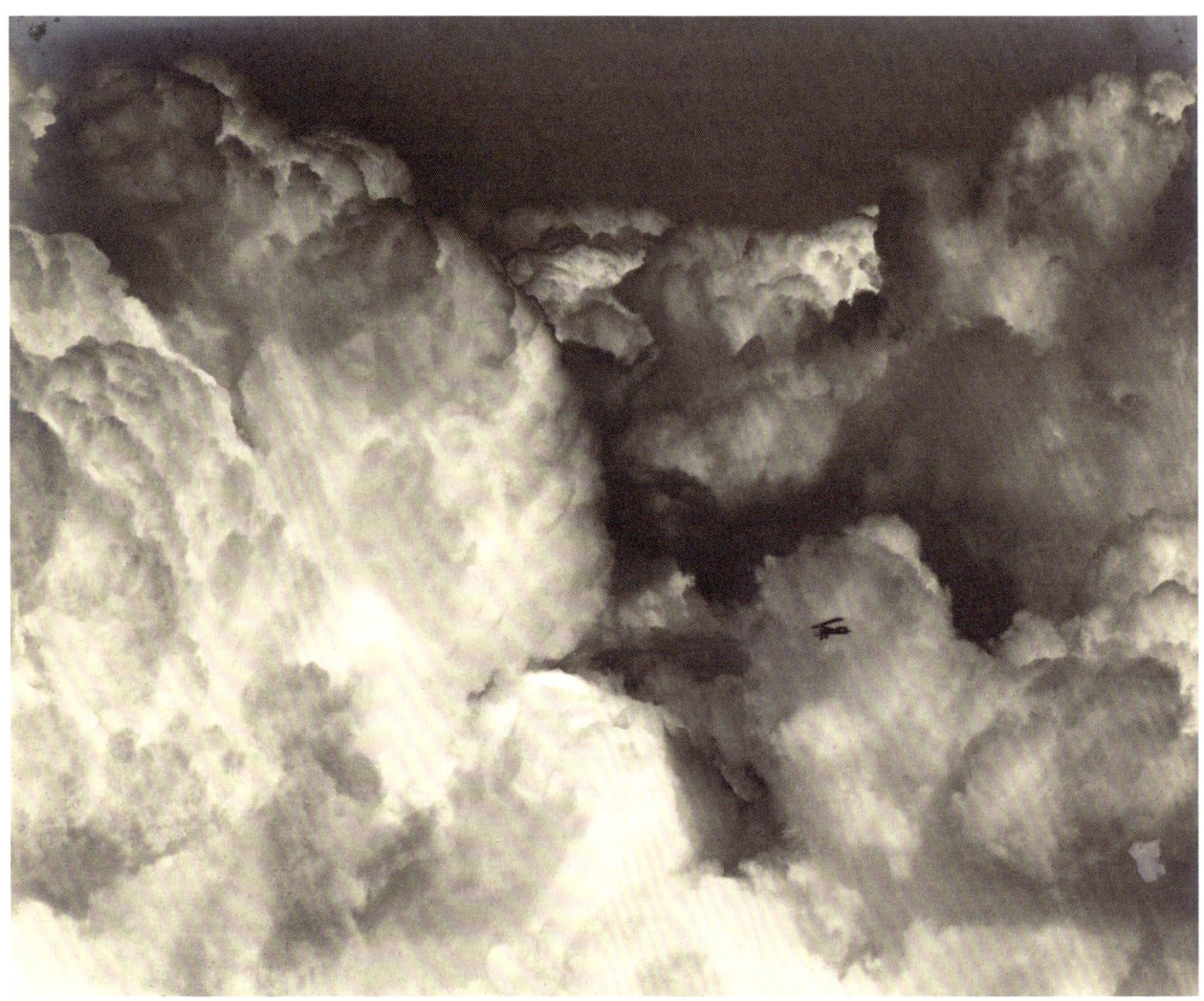

↑
29. *The Storm Centre*, *c.*1920, gelatin
silver print, 40.6 × 51 cm. National
Galleries of Scotland. Purchased
with Art Fund support, 2008

→
30. *Durham*, *c.*1920, gelatin silver
print, 46 × 38 cm. Collection of
Richard and John Buckham

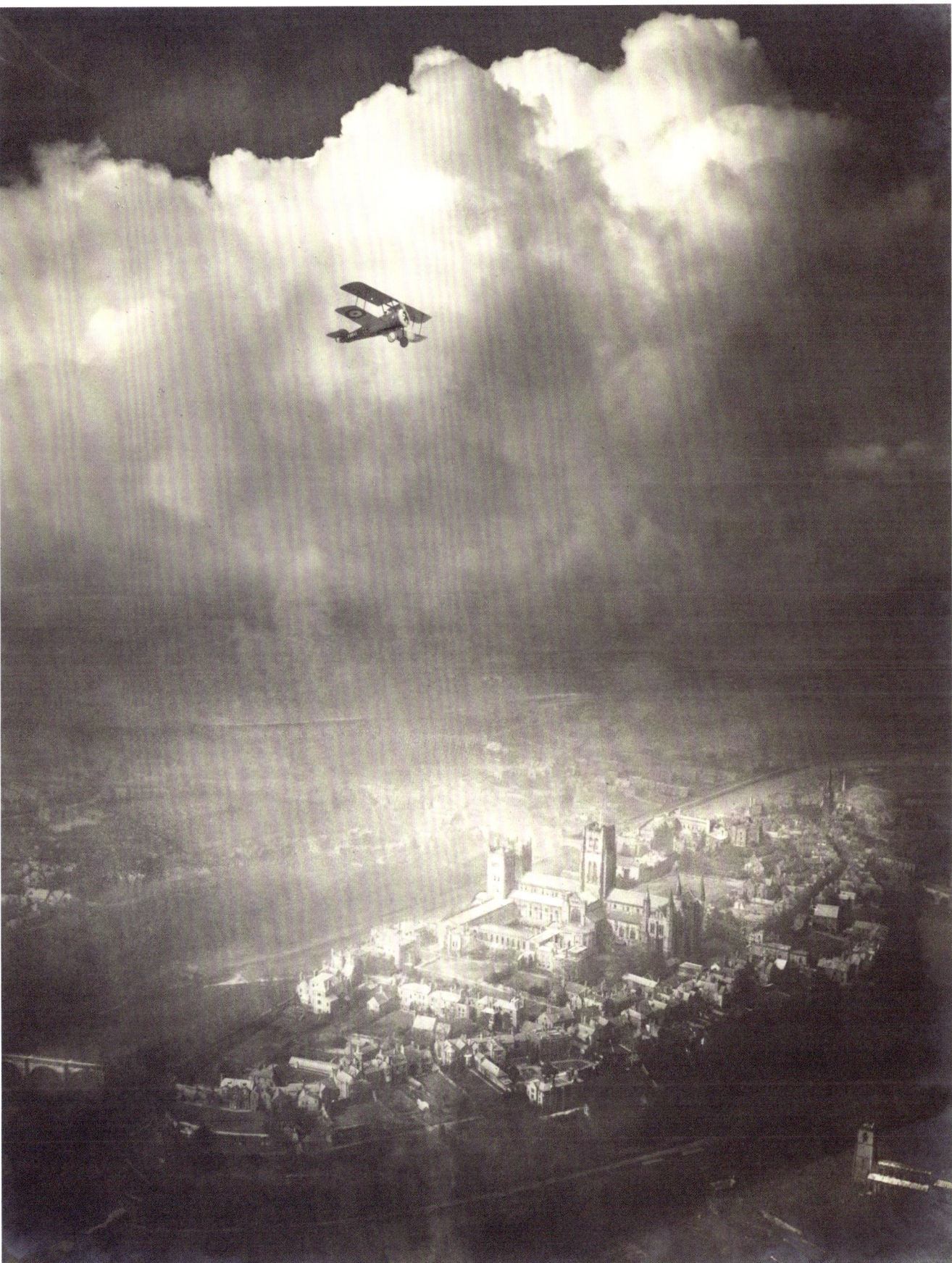

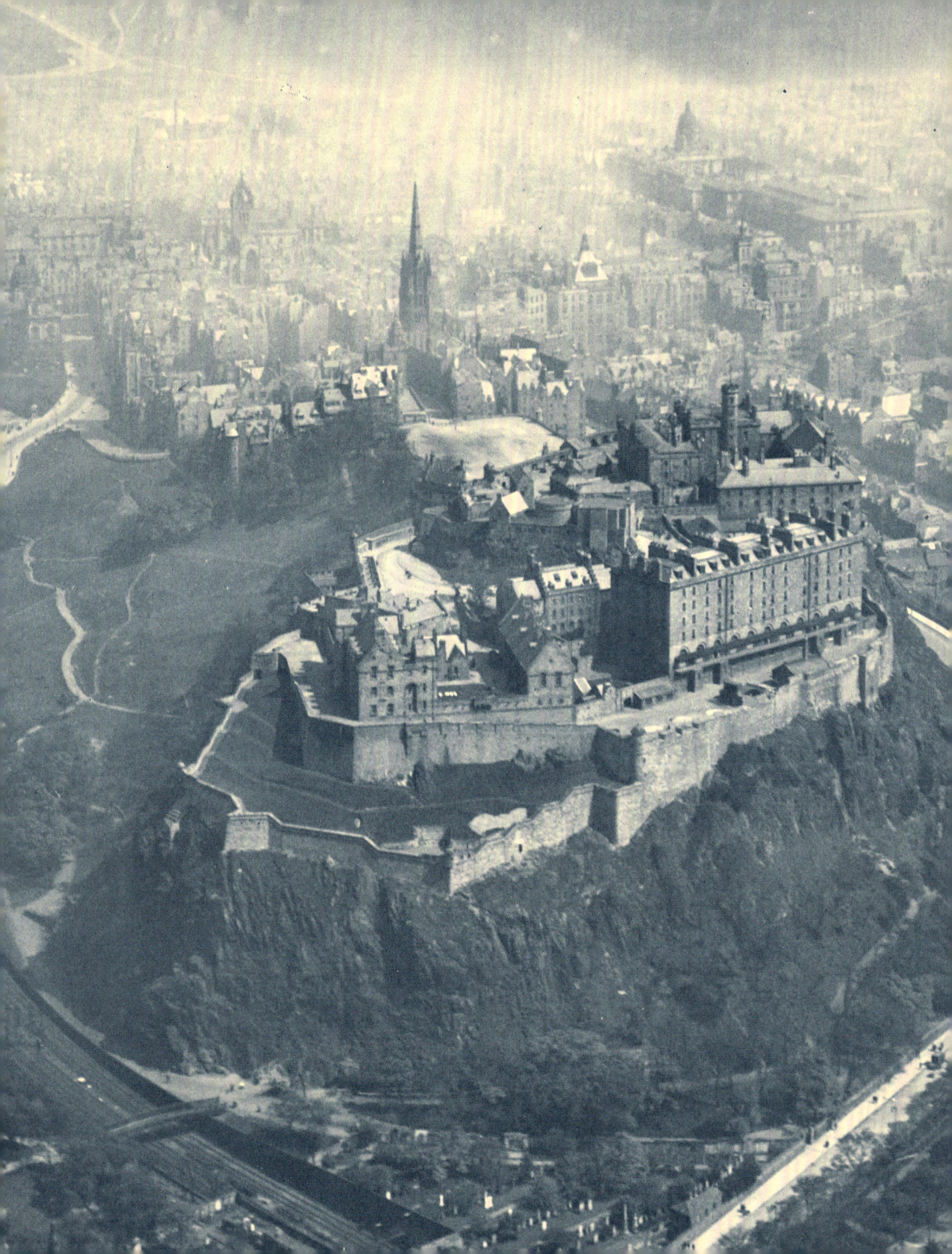

In the Darkroom

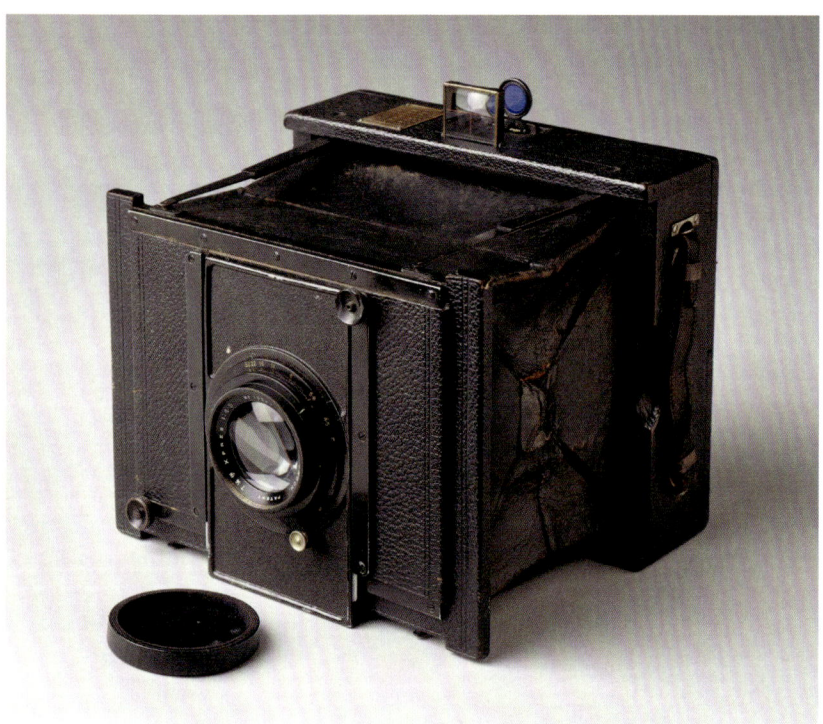

BUCKHAM'S PHOTOGRAPHS are not quite as they seem. At first glance, *The Heart of the Empire* (28) gives the impression that it is a stunning view of London captured from the cockpit of a nearby aeroplane. However, like the majority of his photographs, it is actually a carefully constructed amalgamation of multiple elements.

After the war, Buckham started experimenting with composite photography, where several negatives are used to make one photographic print. This was not a new practice, with nineteenth-century photographers such as the Frenchman Gustave Le Gray (1820–1884) pioneering the technique to combat the problem of the sky requiring a shorter exposure than the land or sea. Buckham built on existing photographic techniques to create a style that was entirely his own. His photographs capture the exhilarating experience of flight, but with a little extra drama.

For Buckham, crafting the perfect composite photograph started with choosing the right camera (31). He rejected the cumbersome cameras that had been developed for aerial photography, preferring to use the more compact models favoured by newspaper reporters that were operated at eye level. He cautioned, however, that the bellows needed to be reinforced with cardboard or aluminium sheets as they are 'not calculated to withstand the force of the mighty gale which sweeps past an aeroplane travelling at something like 100mph'.[1]

↖
31. Alfred Buckham's camera, c.1916, 20 x 24.5 x 21 cm.
National Galleries of Scotland. Purchased from Richard and John Buckham 2019

→
32. *Edinburgh*, c.1920, gelatin silver print, 45.8 × 37.8 cm.
National Galleries of Scotland. Purchased 1990

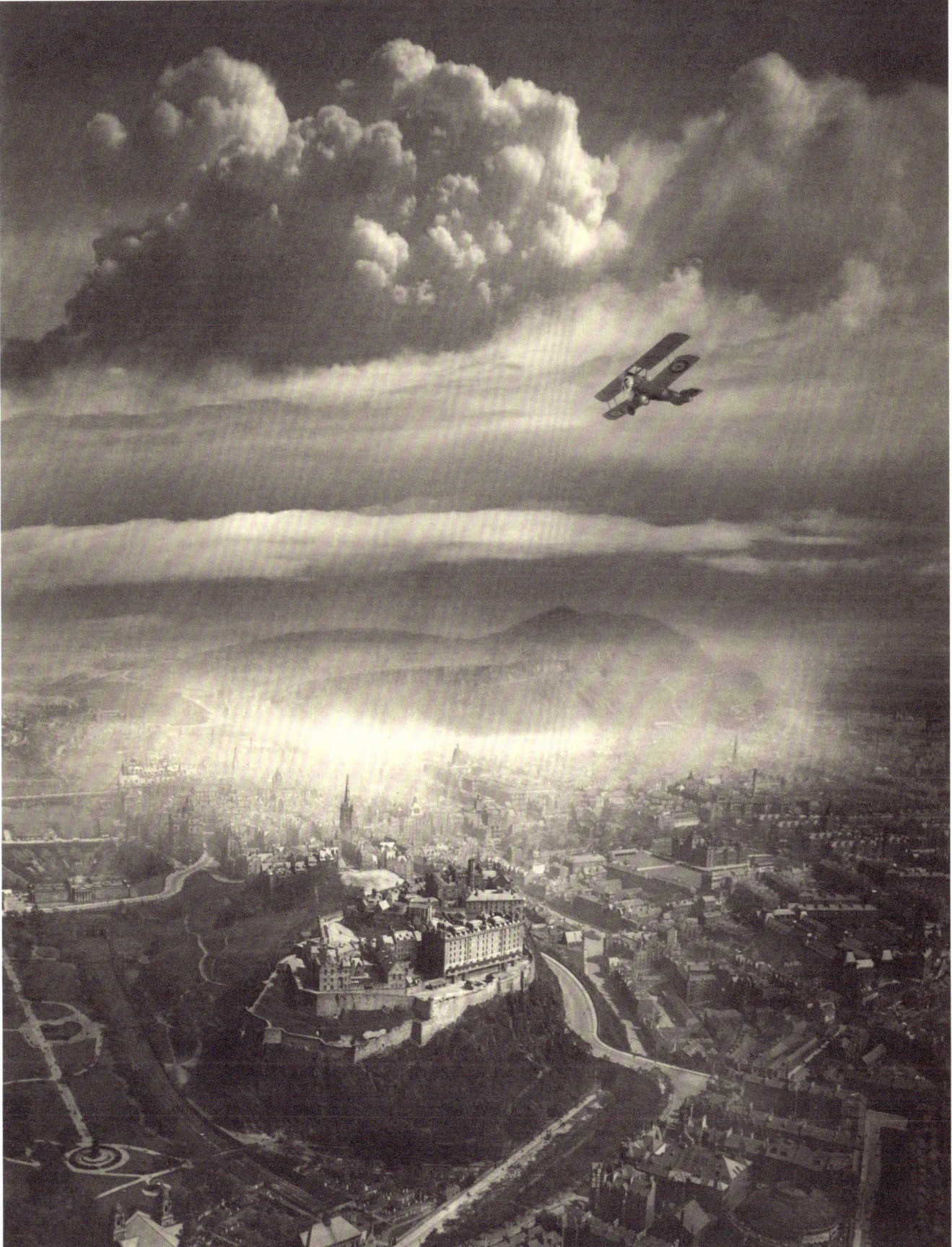

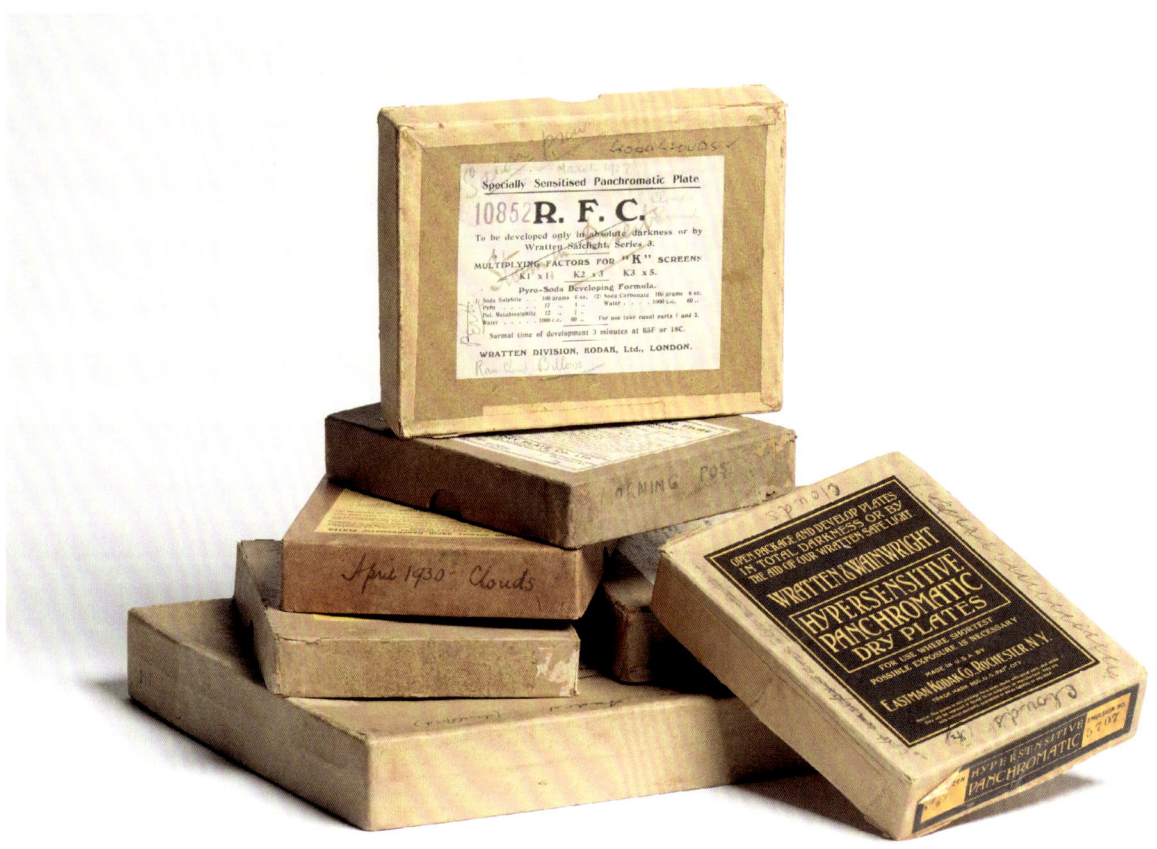

Just as important as the camera was having the resilience and skill to operate it in extreme weather conditions. Buckham recommended that novice aerial photographers 'eschew winter operations; not only because they present greater technical difficulties, but owing to the necessity for working without either goggles or gloves, he would very probably feel somewhat discouraged when his eyelashes froze together and his hands became numbed in a temperature some degrees below zero'.[2]

In a series of articles providing guidance to aspiring aerial photographers he listed a number of key attributes he deemed necessary for success. These included the need to be nimble enough to move easily around the confined space of the cockpit and having the confidence not to hesitate when the perfect moment for a picture presented itself. He was also specific about the best anatomy for his method of aerial photography: 'the camera should be pressed very firmly against one's face, and a pliable nose is a distinct asset when this is being done. Persons with hard, bony and unyielding noses, must make other arrangements'.[3]

↑
33. Negative boxes from Alfred Buckham's cloud library, *c.*1920. Collection of Richard and John Buckham

↗
34. Details of negative boxes from Alfred Buckham's cloud library. Collection of Richard and John Buckham

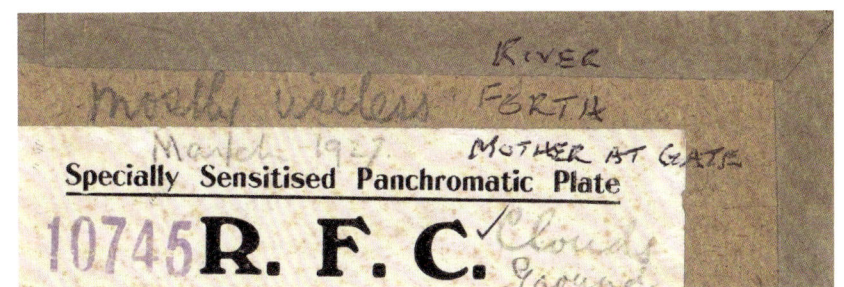

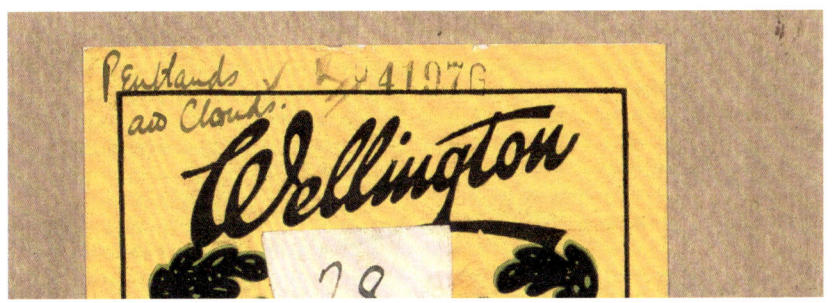

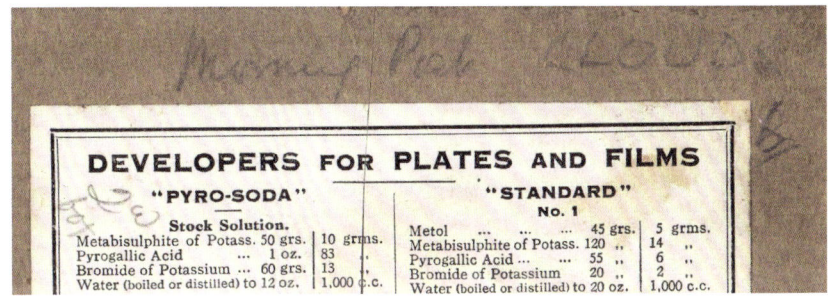

Buckham used glass plate negatives throughout his career, a conscious decision at a time when photographic film was readily available. His preference was for American-made double-coated panchromatic plates, which he discovered, through trial and error, were the most reliable in extreme weather conditions.[4] The detail captured by glass plates was also superior to film, giving him more flexibility in the darkroom.

To fully understand Buckham's unique method of creating composite photographs, it is helpful to examine a particular image in detail. One of his most compelling photographs, *Edinburgh* (32), showing a biplane soaring over Edinburgh Castle, was made with three separate negatives.

The negative Buckham chose as the basis for this photograph depicts an aerial view of the city, with very little sky visible (35). This is because it was near impossible to capture the detail of both the landscape and the clouds in the same negative due to the different exposure times required.

The next stage was to add in the sky, by exposing in quick succession a second negative of perfectly exposed clouds (36). For this purpose, Buckham built an impressive 'cloud library' of over 2,000 negatives (33).

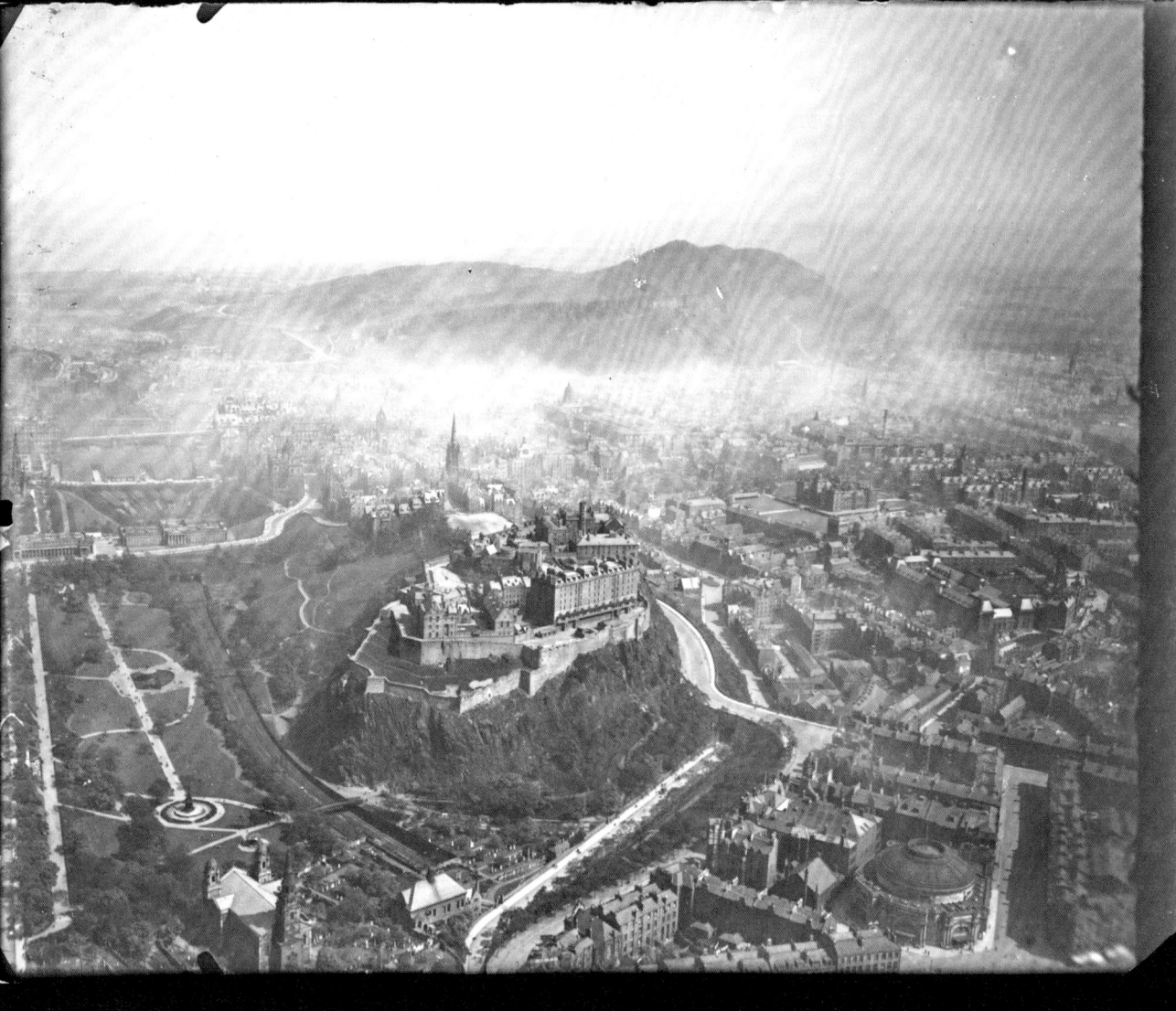

↑
35. *Edinburgh Castle*, *c*.1918,
glass plate negative (positive
reproduction from the original
negative), **10 × 12.5 cm.** National
Galleries of Scotland. Purchased from
Richard and John Buckham 2019

↗
36. *Clouds*, *c*.1918, glass plate
negative (positive reproduction
from the original negative),
13 × 18 cm. National Galleries of
Scotland. Purchased from Richard
and John Buckham 2019

→
37. *Aeroplane*, *c*.1918, glass plate
negative (positive reproduction
from the original negative),
10 × 12.5 cm. National Galleries of
Scotland. Purchased from Richard
and John Buckham 2019

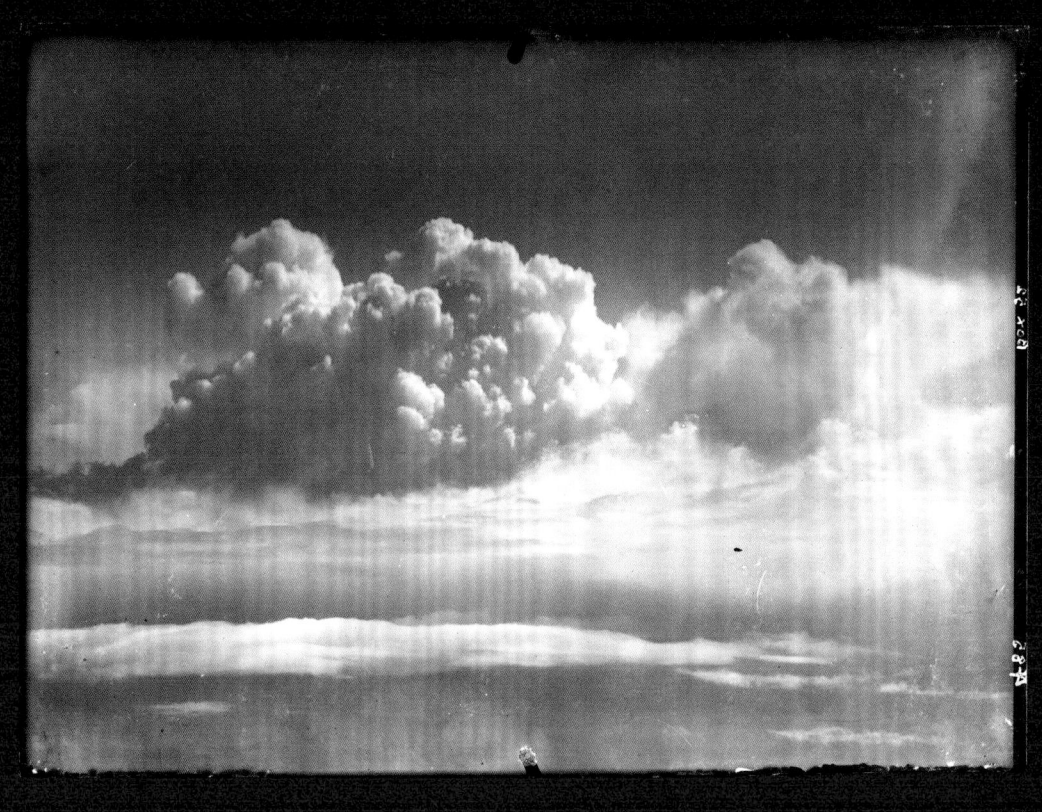

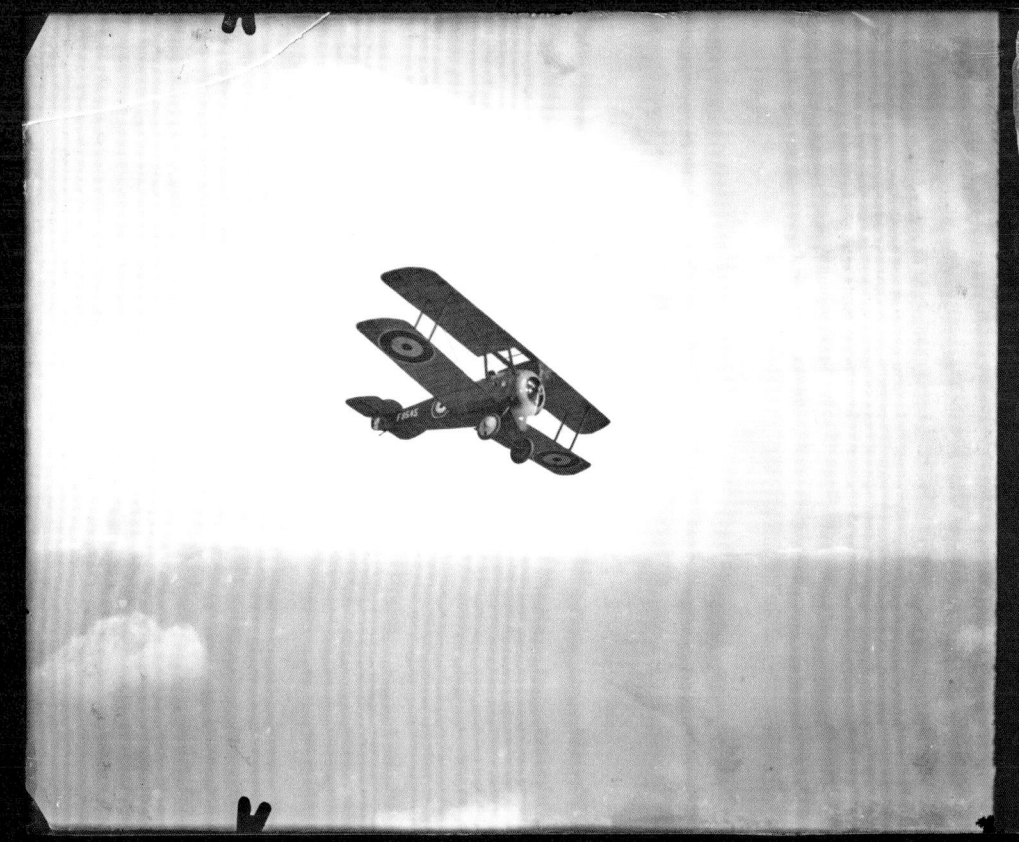

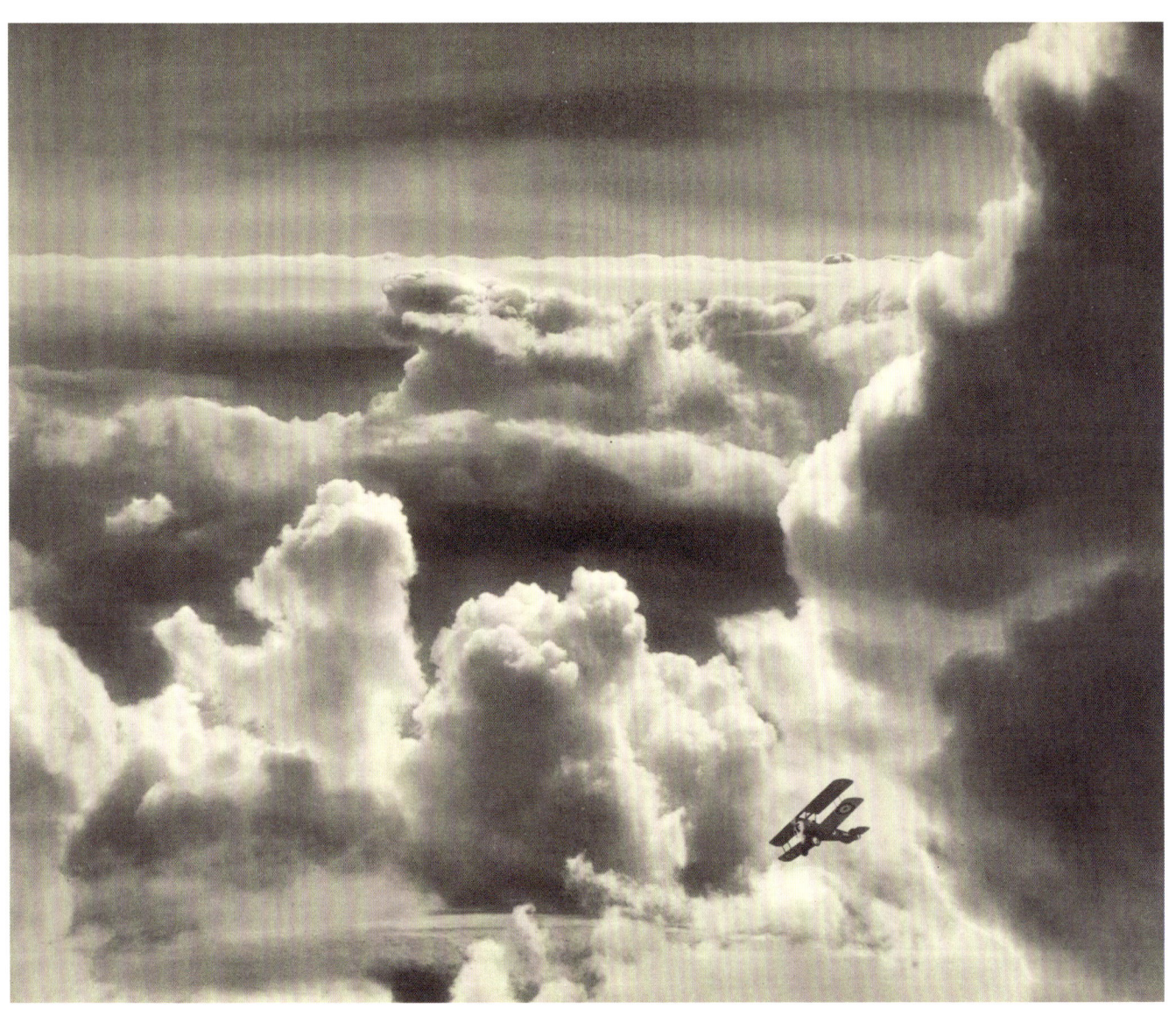

↑
38. *Clouds after a Heavy Thunderstorm*, *c.*1920, gelatin silver print, 37.8 × 46.2 cm.
Collection of Richard and John Buckham

→
39. *Auld Reekie*, *c.*1920, gelatin silver print, 45.3 × 37.7 cm.
National Galleries of Scotland. Purchased from Richard and John Buckham 2019

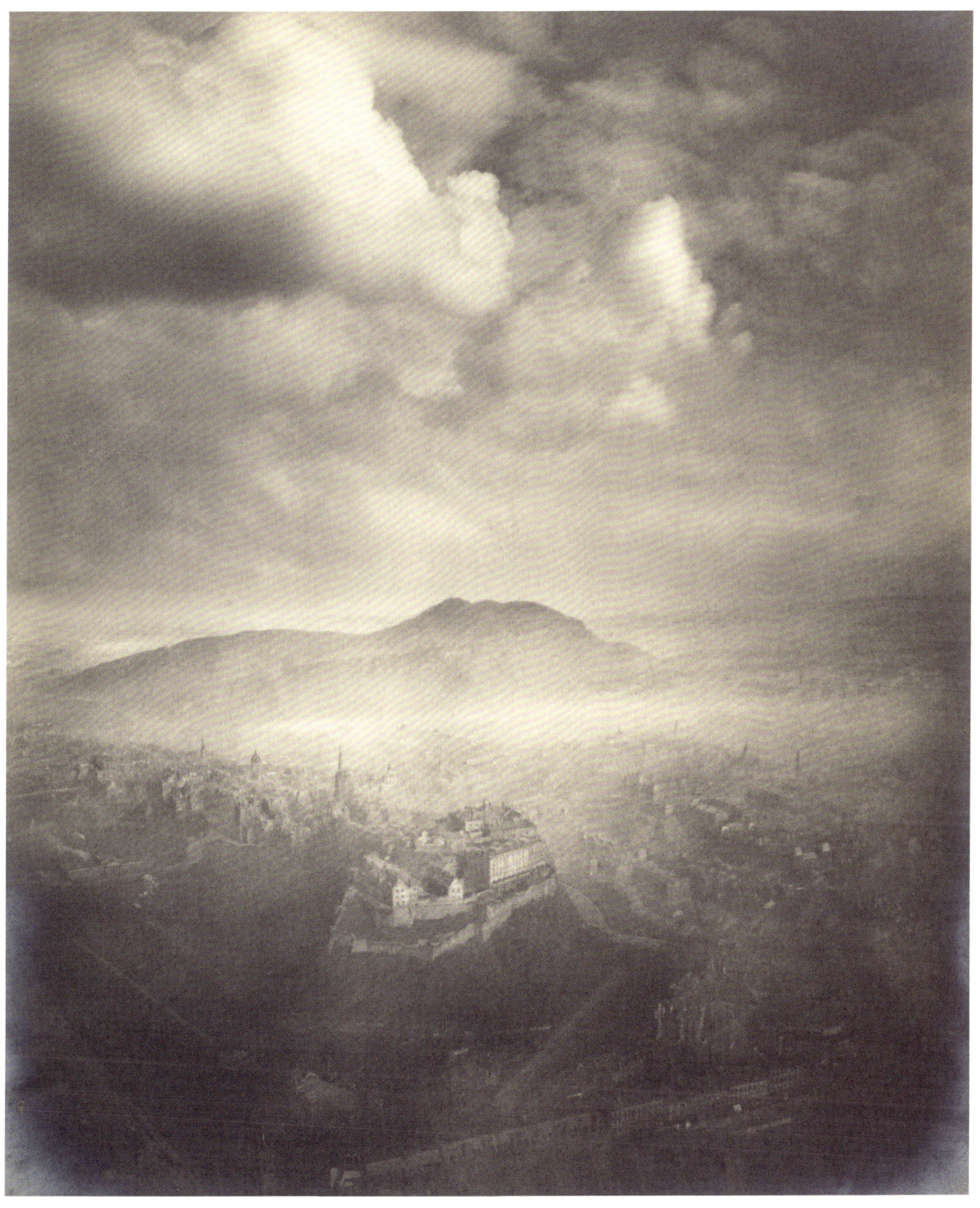

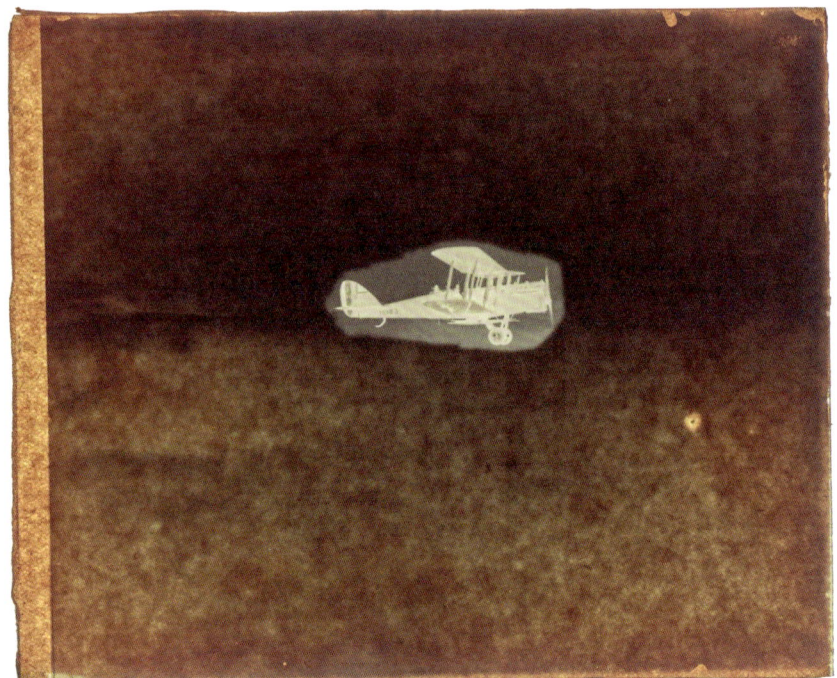

These were diligently catalogued with helpful reference notes such as 'good clouds' and 'mostly useless'. This was the most delicate part of the process, with the wrong choice ruining the final composition:

And here is just where the hasty or unobservant worker may go badly astray, producing incredible or even appalling results. For the lighting of the landscape must be in correct relation to the light coming down from the sky, and heavy cloud masses insist that they shall have corresponding shapes upon the earth.[5]

Selecting the right negative sometimes required inspecting fifty or more, and occasionally Buckham created more interesting cloud formations by taping two negatives together (47).[6]

Some work was then required to soften the horizon where the two negatives met. This was partly done in the darkroom, using a 'dodging' technique to lighten the exposure of some areas and a 'burning' effect to darken others. Buckham also used chemical reducers and stumping chalk on the final print to bring the whole into harmony. In the photograph *Edinburgh*, the effect of the light below Arthur's Seat has been adjusted to better match the clouds above.

A unique characteristic of Buckham's photographs is the aeroplanes that provide a focal point to the image. These also came from a store of negatives, where the original background was masked out. Buckham

↖
40. *Aeroplane*, *c.*1918, **glass plate negative, 10 × 12.5 cm.** National Galleries of Scotland. Purchased from Richard and John Buckham 2019

↗
41. *Cloud Turrets*, *c.*1918, **gelatin silver print, 38 × 45.7 cm.** National Galleries of Scotland. Purchased with Art Fund support, 2008

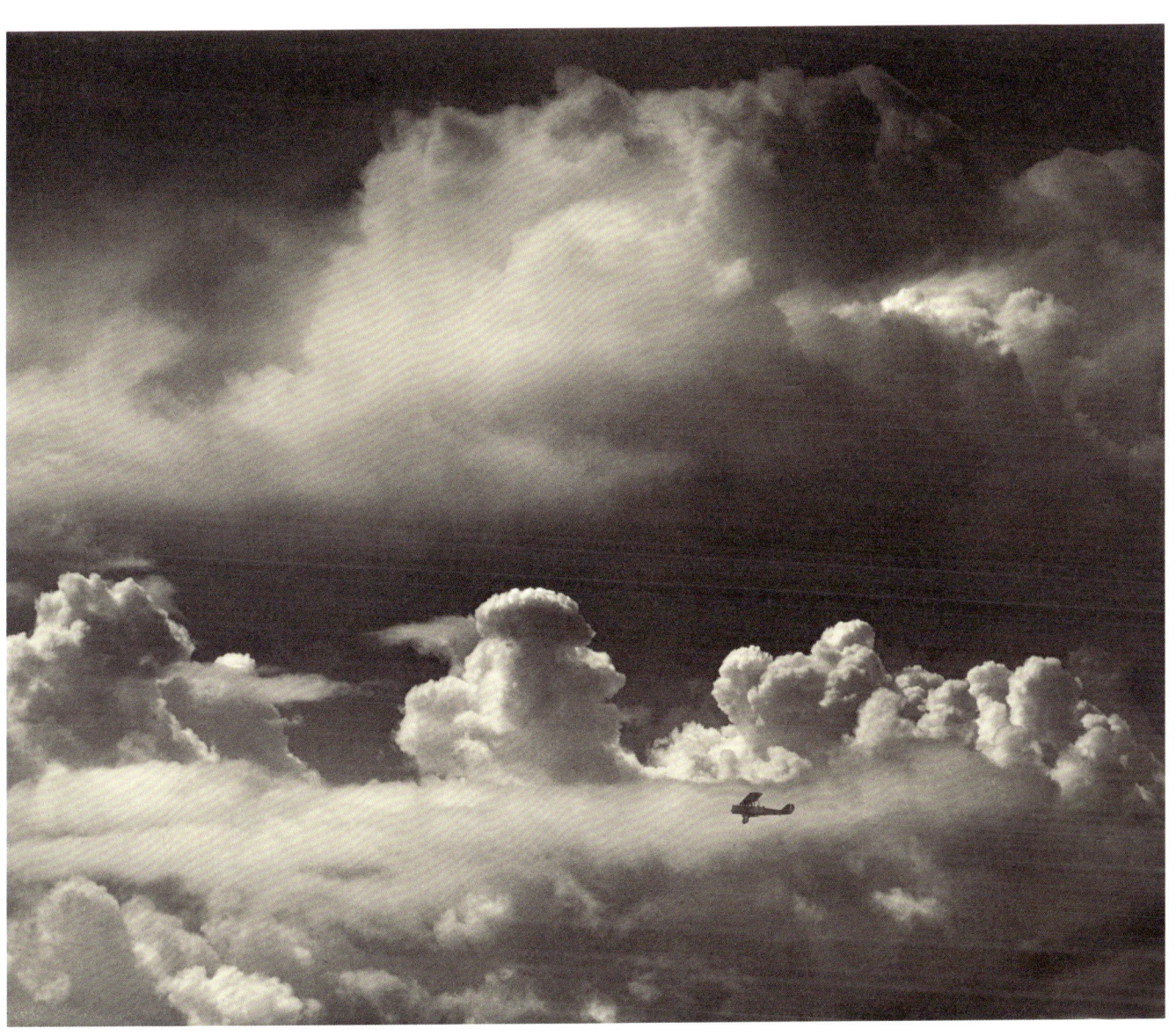

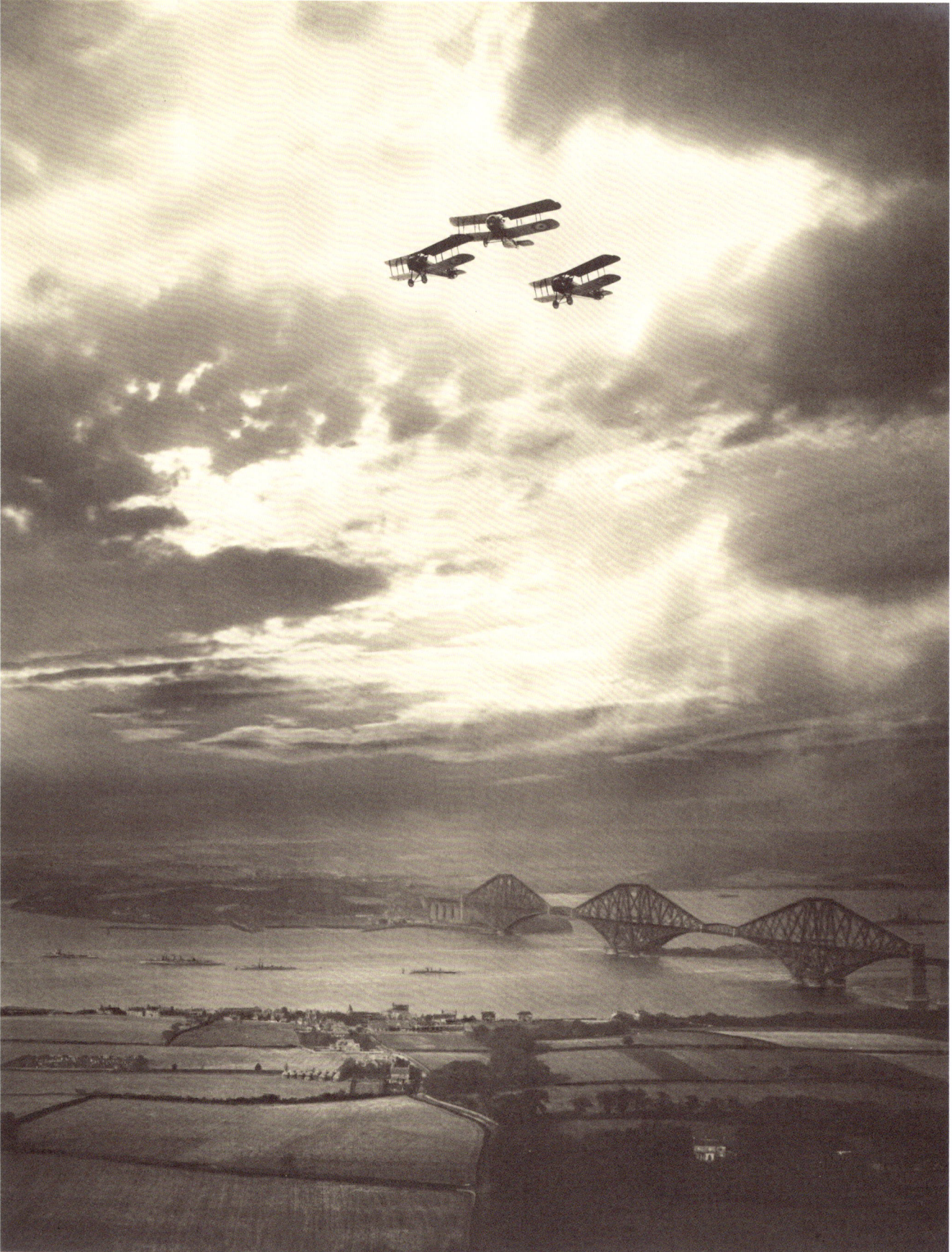

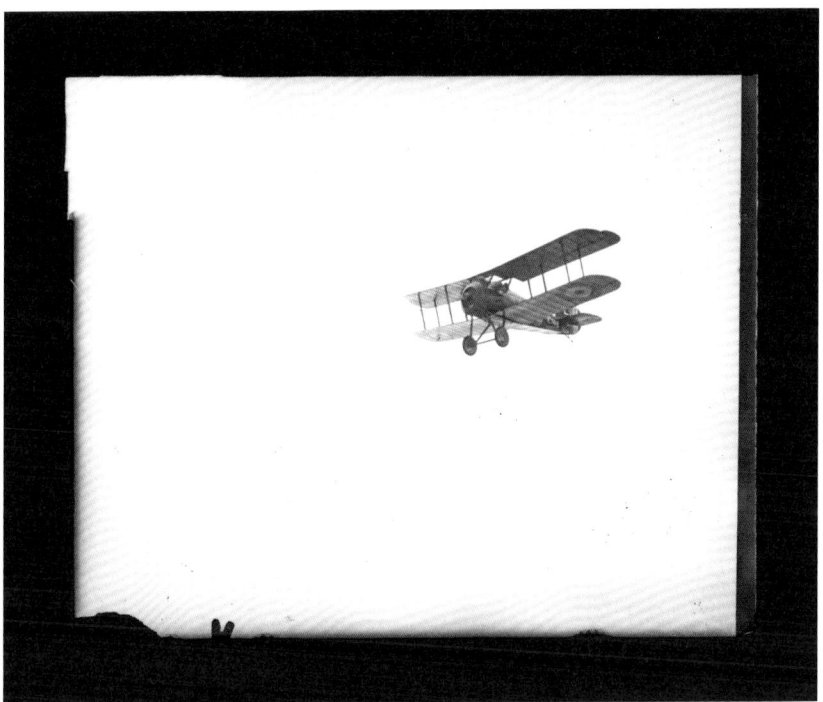

identified a light area of the print to add the aeroplane and used a pin mark to help him expose the negative in the right position. He would also have used an enlarger to match the scale of the aeroplane to the landscape, making the scene appear realistic.

All of these aeroplanes were photographed on the ground, as it would not have been possible to photograph a moving aircraft from a similarly speedy vehicle. Buckham wanted it to appear that these aeroplanes were in flight, so on occasion he painted in the dents on the bottom of the wheels that gave away that the aeroplane was still in the airfield.

To allow him to reuse negatives, Buckham rarely edited them by scratching out or filling in areas, as was common for photographers using glass plates. Instead, he made all of his final adjustments in the print. In the *Edinburgh* photograph he uses black watercolour to enhance the contrast between the brooding castle and the rest of the city, and scratches back to the white paper to show the light glinting on key landmarks. This final stage of the process ensured that every photograph is unique.

Buckham's method of composite photography meant that several versions of the same scene could exist. *Auld Reekie* (39) also takes Edinburgh as the basis for the final print, but the city is paired with a different set of cloud formations. The other notable difference is the absence of the aeroplane in *Auld Reekie*, which shifts the scene from dynamic to pensive.

←
42. *The Forth Bridge*, *c.*1920, **gelatin silver print, 40.4 × 32.4 cm.** Collection of Richard and John Buckham

↗
43. *Aeroplane*, *c.*1918, **glass plate negative (positive reproduction from the original negative), 10 × 12.5 cm.** National Galleries of Scotland. Purchased from Richard and John Buckham 2019

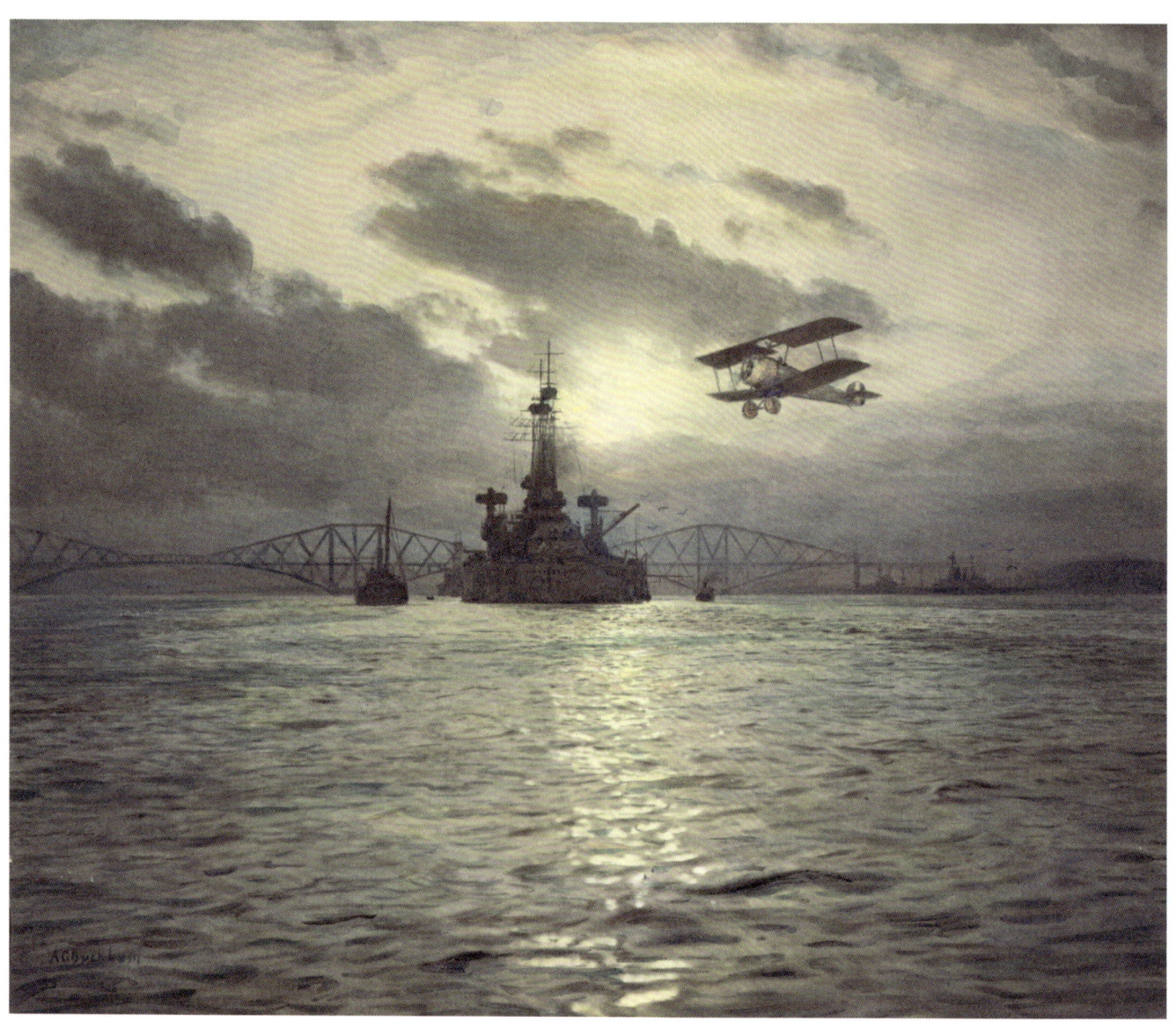

↑
**44. *USS* Wyoming *in the Firth
of Forth*, 1918, hand-coloured
gelatin silver print, 33.5 × 40 cm.**
Collection of Richard and
John Buckham

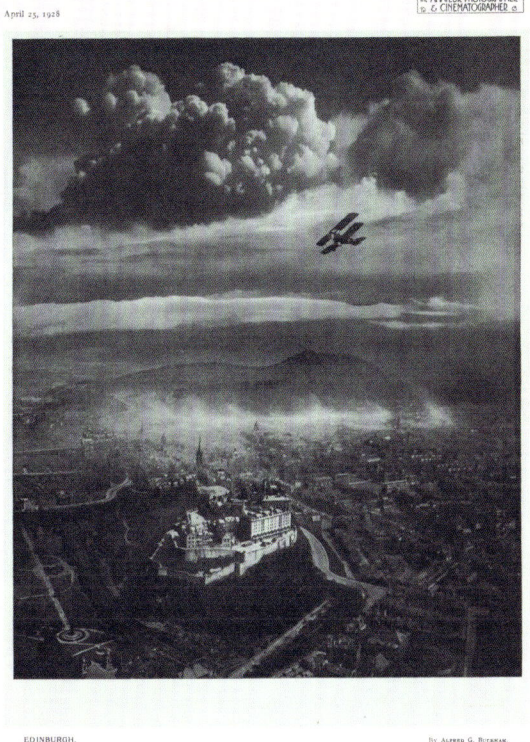
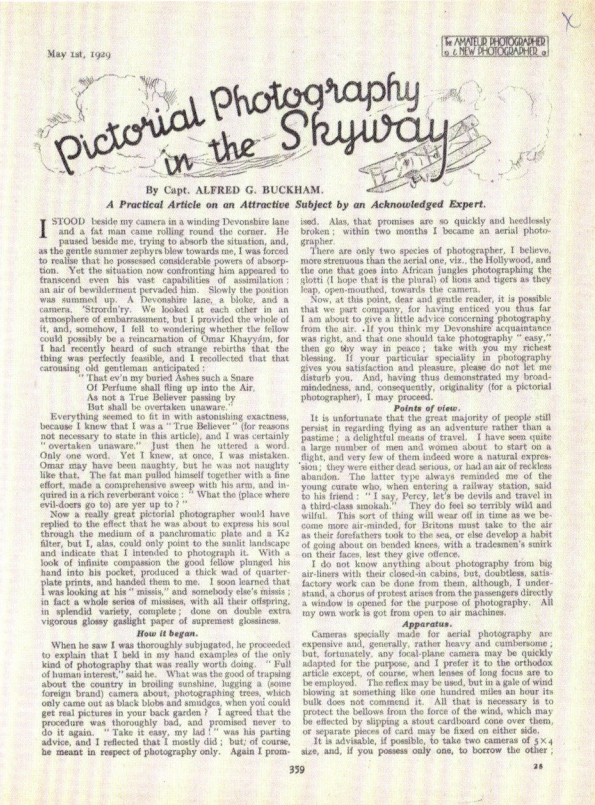

The same aeroplanes appear in multiple prints. The negative used for *Edinburgh* (32) was clearly a favourite from his library, with the biplane also featuring in *Clouds after a Heavy Thunderstorm* (38) and several other photographs, sometimes flipped or scaled up or down.

Occasionally, Buckham even went as far as printing the same aeroplane multiple times in one photograph. Two of the biplanes in *The Forth Bridge* (42) were taken from the same negative (43). This photograph is far more easily recognisable as a composite image because the aeroplanes are flying too close together and at impossible angles.

He also experimented with hand colouring his photographs, probably still harbouring some of his earlier aspiration to be a painter. *USS Wyoming in the Firth of Forth* (44), depicting light breaking through dramatic clouds to frame a great warship, is certainly reminiscent of Turner's atmospheric painting *Sea View* (1).

Buckham's innovation in the darkroom intrigued his contemporaries, and he was invited to contribute articles to multiple photography journals including *Camera Craft* and the *Amateur Photographer*. The advice he gave to his fellow photographers is generous and full of his characteristic warmth and humour. These articles testify that he was proud of the artistry of his photographs, never hiding that they were composite images.

↑
45. *Amateur Photographer*, 25 April 1928 and 1 May 1929, 27.2 × 21.1 cm. Collection of Richard and John Buckham

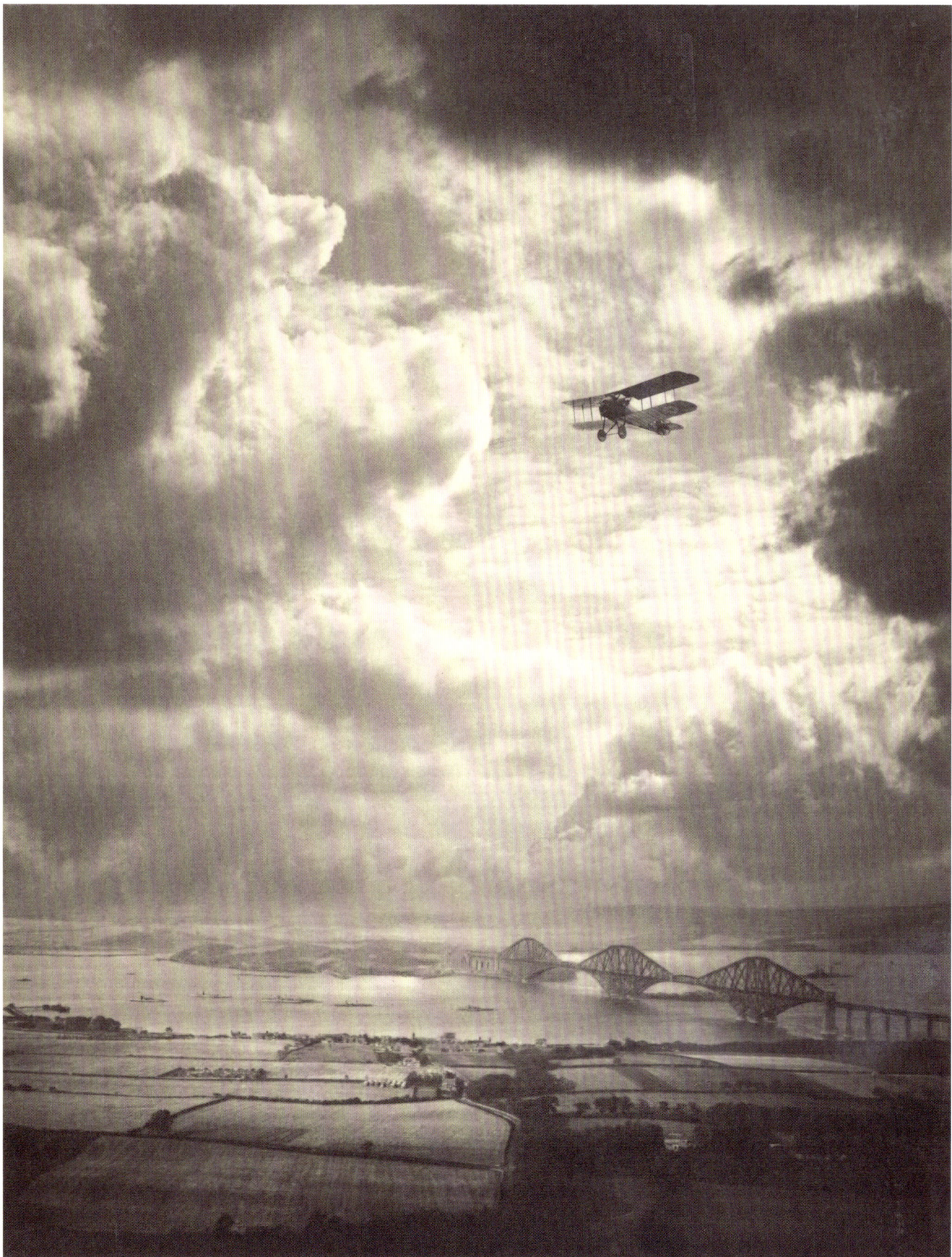

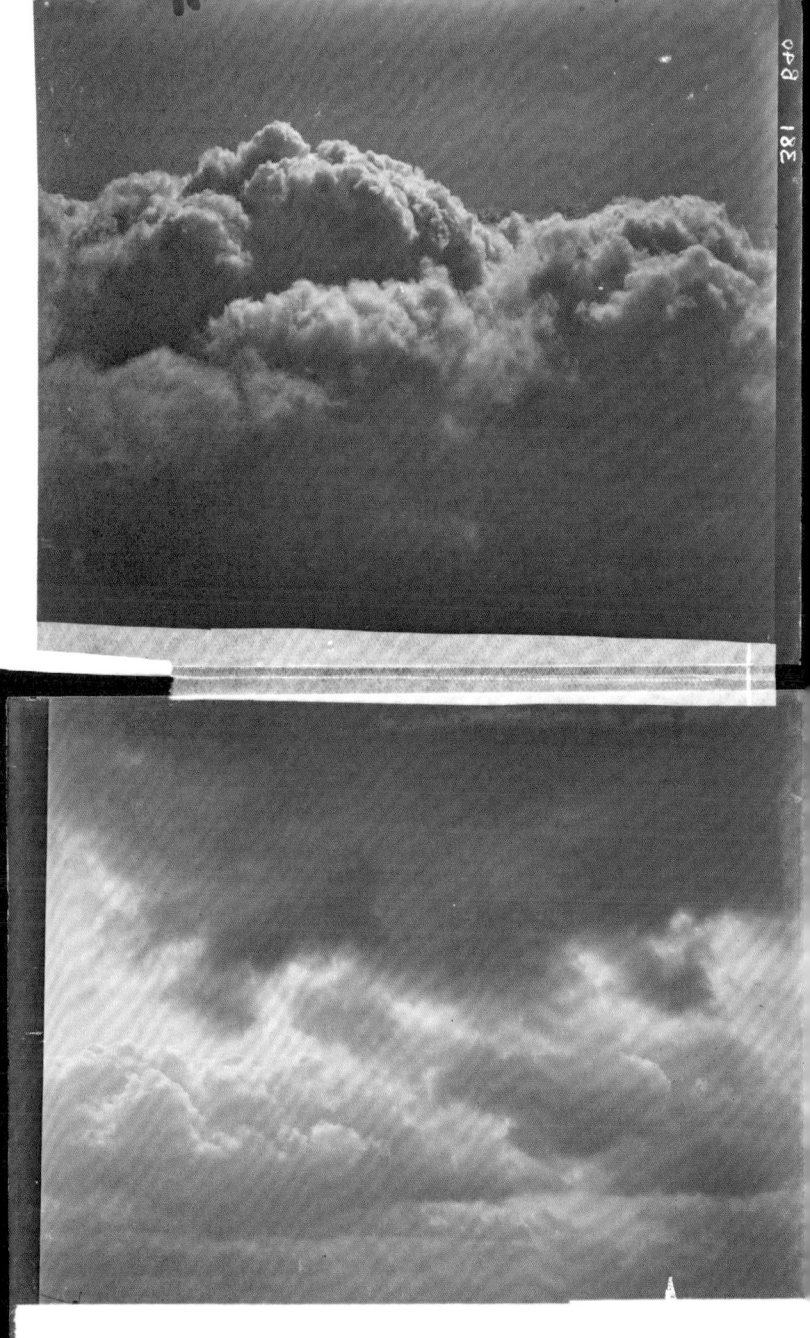

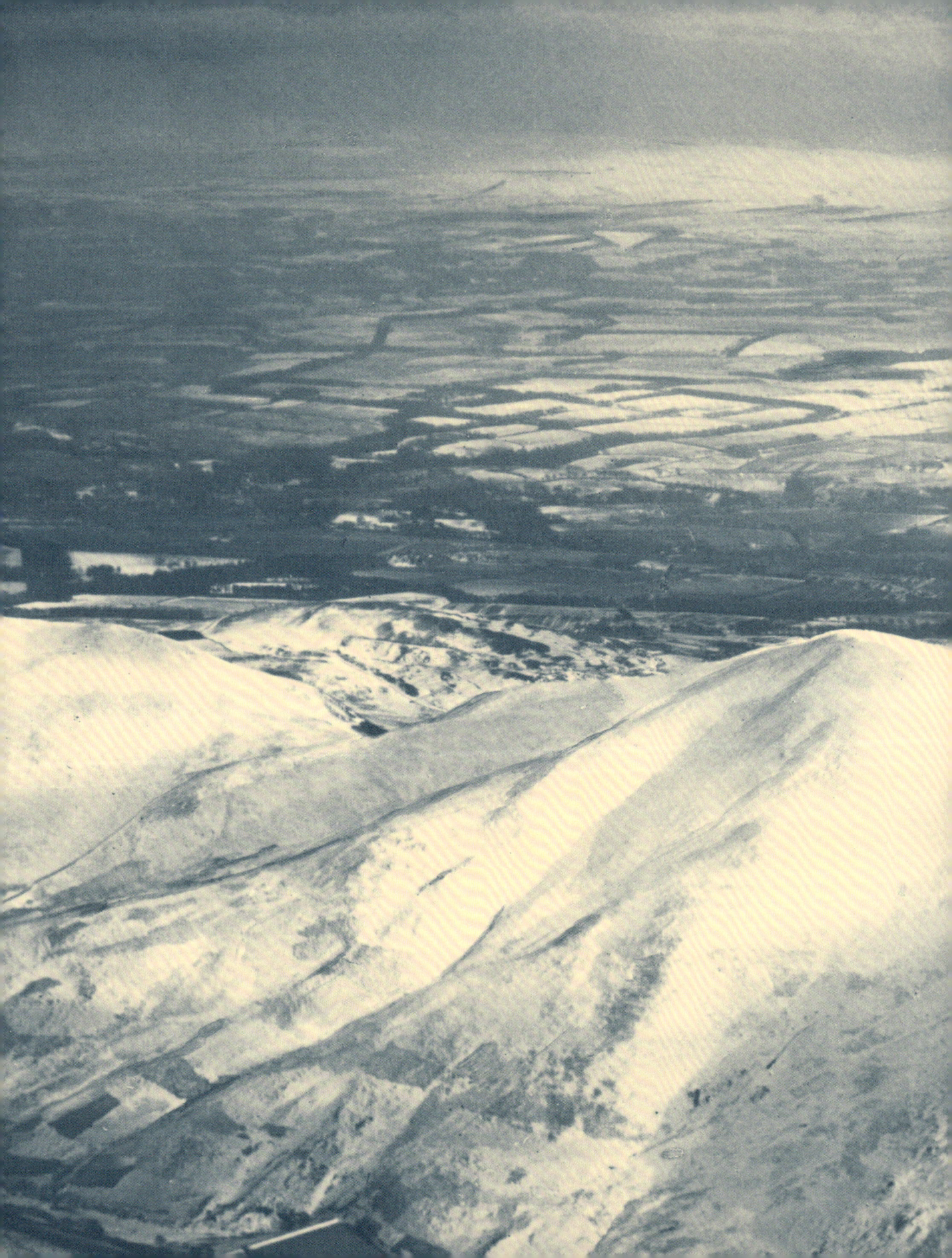

In Scotland

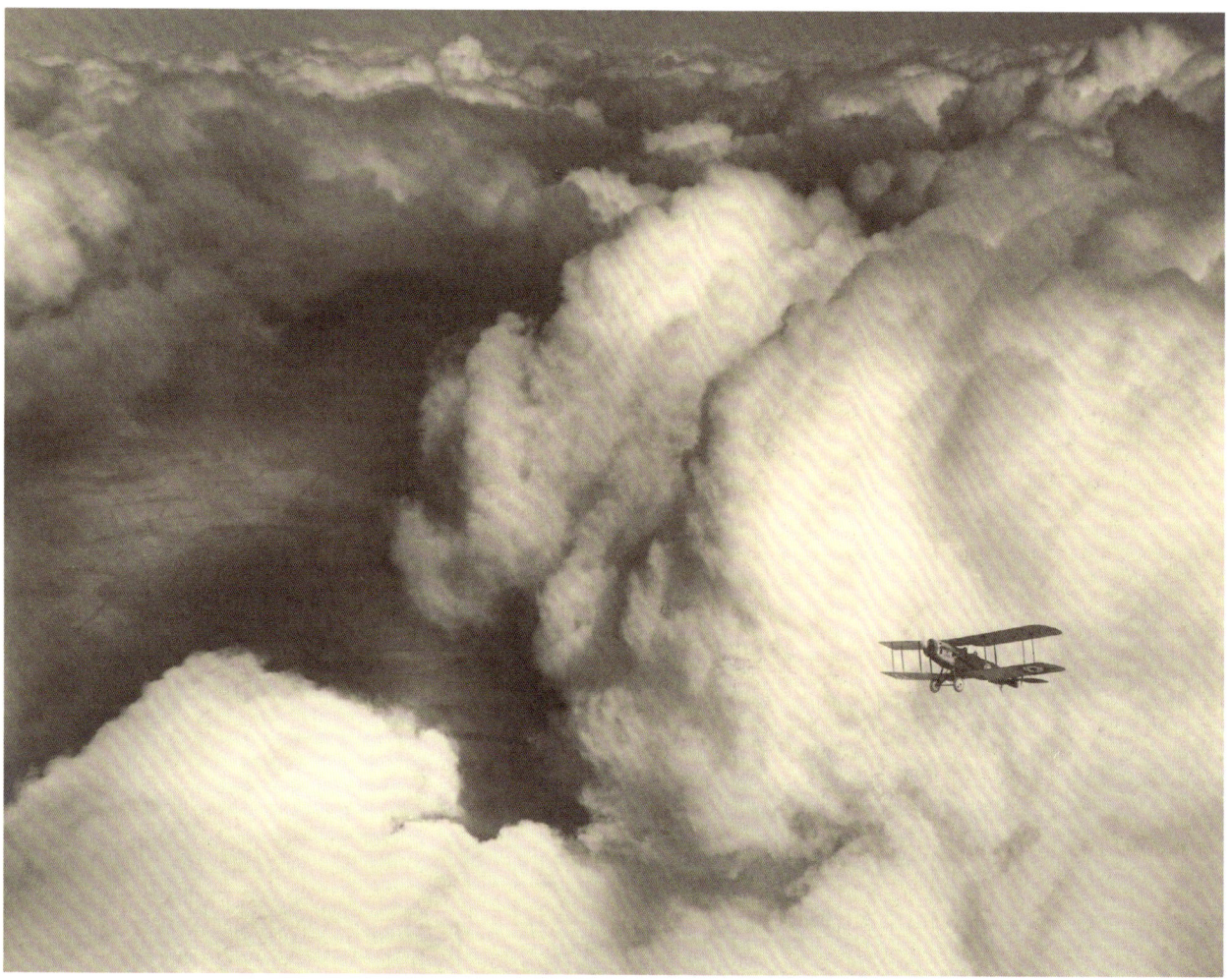

FROM HIS BASE at RAF Turnhouse, just outside Edinburgh, Buckham explored Scotland from the sky. The negatives he made in Scotland formed the basis of his early experiments in the darkroom, and place Edinburgh and the surrounding area centre stage in his photographs. The magnificent historic architecture of the capital, snow-capped peaks of the nearby Pentland Hills and picturesque coastline of the Firth of Forth all provided a dramatic backdrop for his spellbinding images. In creating composite photographs, Buckham was seeking to convey the exhilaration of flying over these unique landscapes. Speaking of his photograph *Edinburgh* (32) he said:

I have a certain fondness, too, for this print, because it presents, so nearly, the effect that I saw. There is a wonderful charm about Edinburgh, especially when viewed from the air, and although I have flown some hundreds of times over the city, there is always some new aspect to be seen or fresh charm discovered.[1]

↑
48. *The Orkney Islands, Altitude 6,000 feet*, 1910s, printed c.1918, **gelatin silver print , 30.2 × 37.7 cm.**
Metropolitan Museum of Art, New York. Gift of Clarence McK. Lewis, 1954

→
49. *Phoebus 'gins to rise*, c.1920, **gelatin silver print, 45.8 × 38 cm.**
National Galleries of Scotland. Purchased with Art Fund support, 2008

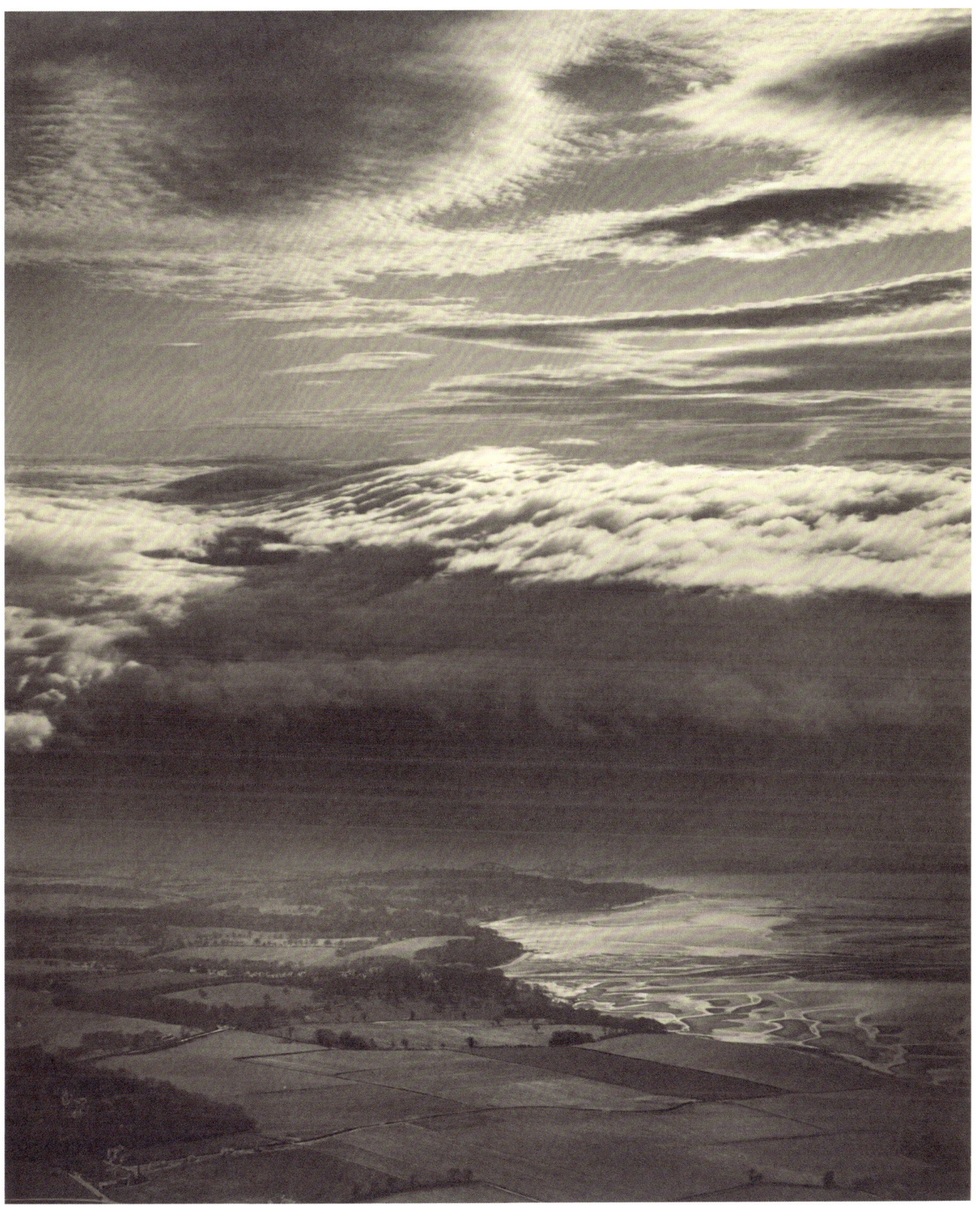

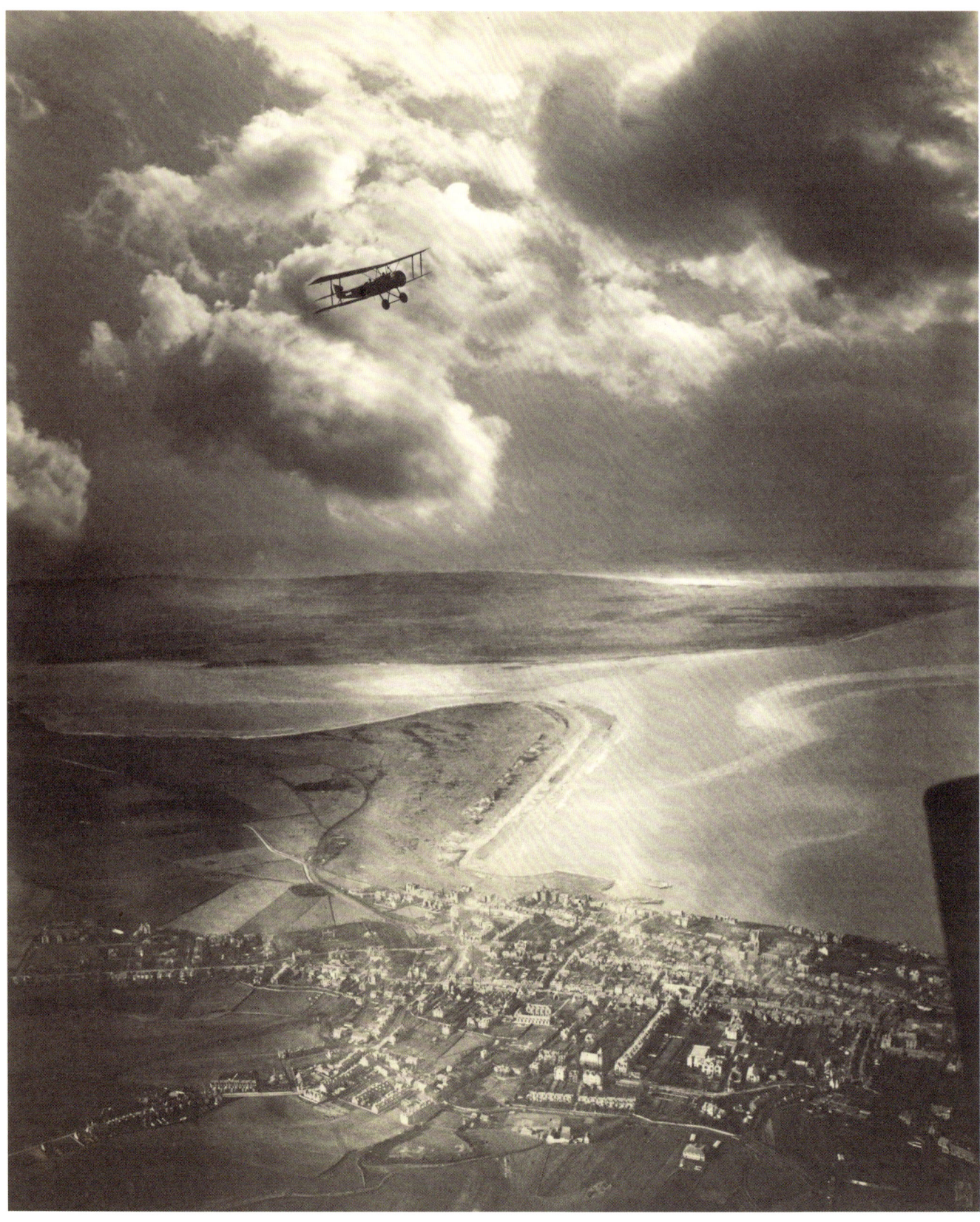

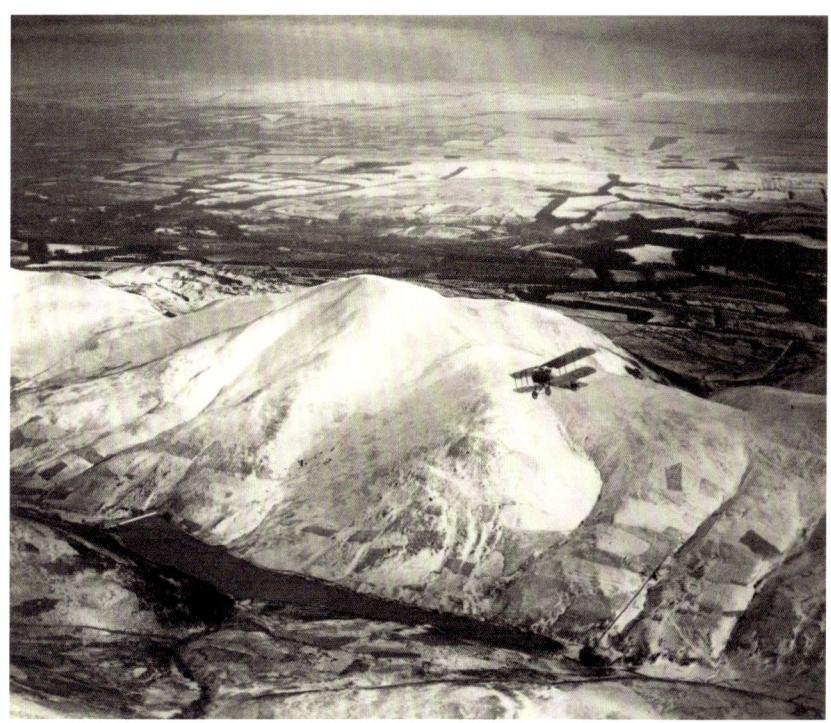

50. *St Andrews and the Famous
Golf Links*, *c*.1920, gelatin silver
print, 45.2 × 37.7 cm. Collection of
Richard and John Buckham

51. *Winter Treads on the
Pentlands*, *c*.1920, gelatin silver
print, 38.2 × 45.8 cm. Collection
of Richard and John Buckham

Buckham photographed historic Scottish landmarks including St Andrews, Linlithgow Palace and the National Wallace Monument in Stirling. These aerial views provide a new perspective on familiar places. His photograph of St Andrews, showing the world-renowned Old Course, gives golfers an insight into the layout of the famous links (50). This picture was reproduced by the *Illustrated London News* in an article about golf, declaring that Buckham's photograph should be 'of unusual interest to all golfers, giving, as it does, a view of the famous course from an entirely new and unusual angle'.[2]

He was clearly interested in Scotland's rich history, often annotating the reverse of his photographs with snippets of information and observations. He recorded that the small octagonal turret visible in his photograph of Linlithgow Palace (59) was alleged to be where Margaret, the consort of King James IV, awaited his return from the Battle of Flodden in 1513. The romance of Mary, Queen of Scots, being imprisoned on a tiny island in Loch Leven in 1567 captured the imagination of British lifestyle magazine *Tatler*, which published Buckham's photograph of the isolated fortress (58) in its January 1931 edition.[3]

Buckham twice attempted to photograph industrial Glasgow.[4] Although he was used to flying in challenging conditions, the dense smoke that engulfed the city made it impossible to secure a clear image.

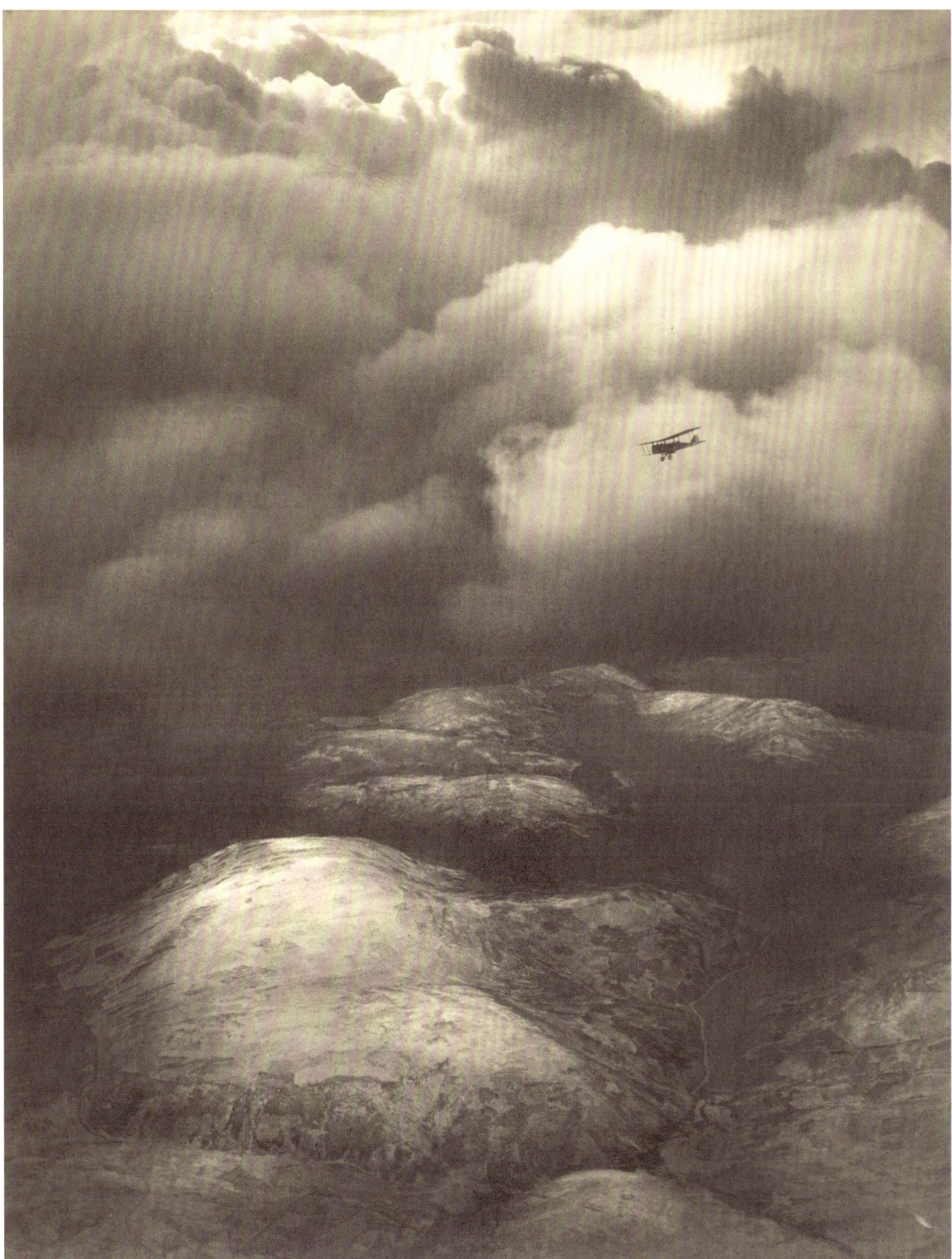

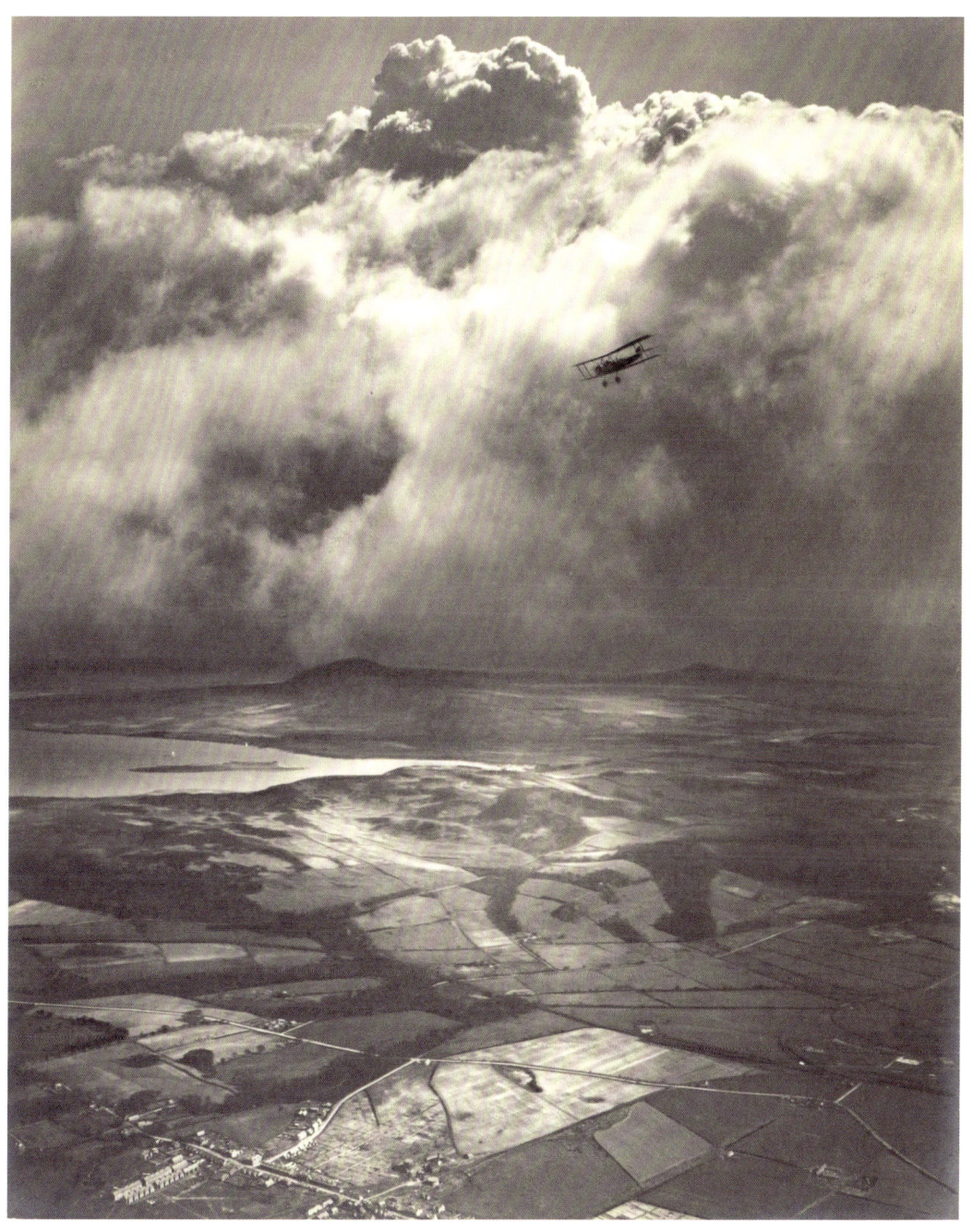

← 52. *Uplands. Snowstorm Passing*, c.1920, gelatin silver print, 46 × 38 cm. National Galleries of Scotland. Purchased with Art Fund support, 2008

↑ 53. *Loch Leven*, c.1920, gelatin silver print, 46 × 38 cm. Collection of Richard and John Buckham

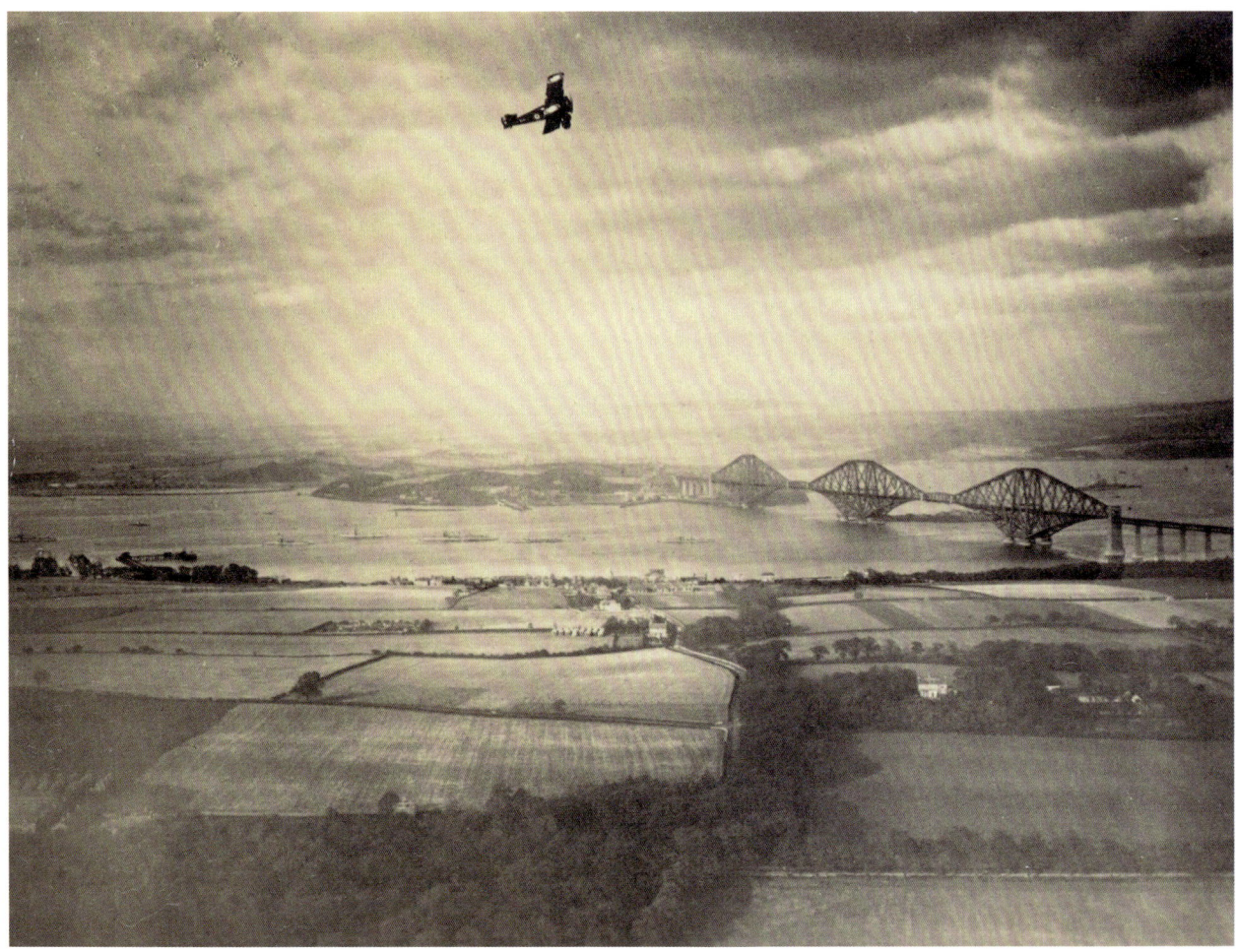

This was a predicament that frustrated Buckham throughout his career. Speaking at a conference on smoke and aviation in 1935, he revealed that he had once been involved in a military experiment to ascertain if there was a combination of plate and filter that would penetrate city smog. Although some success was found above other Scottish cities in the summer months, he came to the glum conclusion that 'the people of Leith [Edinburgh] breathe almost undiluted smoke during about four months of the year'.[5]

He had more success in the fresh air of the Pentlands, which he photographed on multiple occasions. Some of these images appear to be faithful depictions of the landscape but have in fact been flipped to better match Buckham's artistic vision. *Sunset over the Pentland Range* (57) shows an inverse of the hillside photographed, but this liberty is forgiven when presented with the spectacular final image where the voluminous clouds flawlessly mirror the contours of the hills below.

As is evident in the previous chapter, Buckham photographed the Forth Bridge more than any other landmark. This icon of Scottish

↑
54. RAF Turnhouse Christmas card, 1918, gelatin silver print, 14.3 × 17.7 cm. National Galleries of Scotland. Gift of the Bartholomew Family, Edinburgh, 2022

→
55. *Sunshine, Wind and Rain*, **c.1920, gelatin silver print, 46.2 × 37.8 cm.** National Galleries of Scotland. Purchased with Art Fund support, 2008

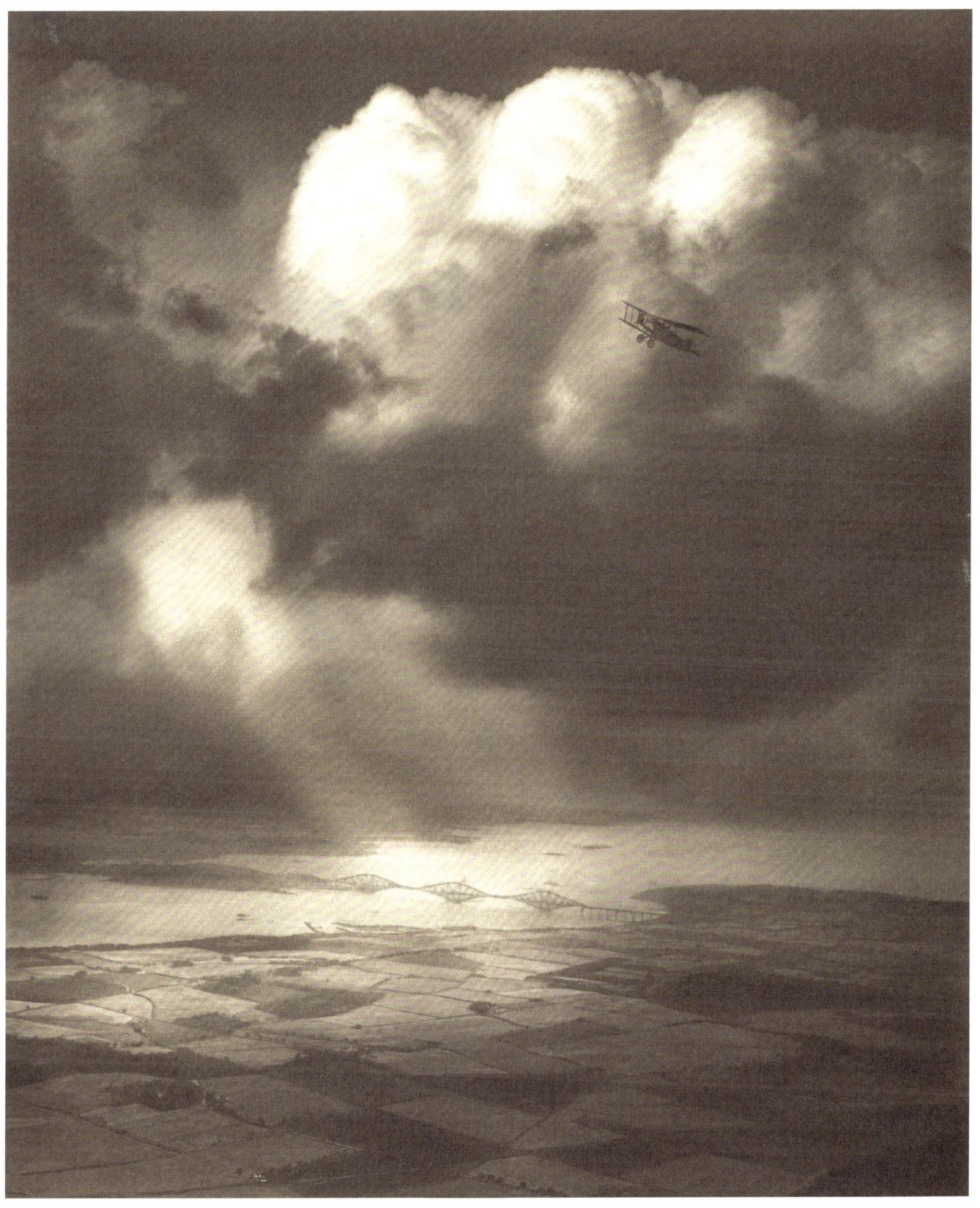

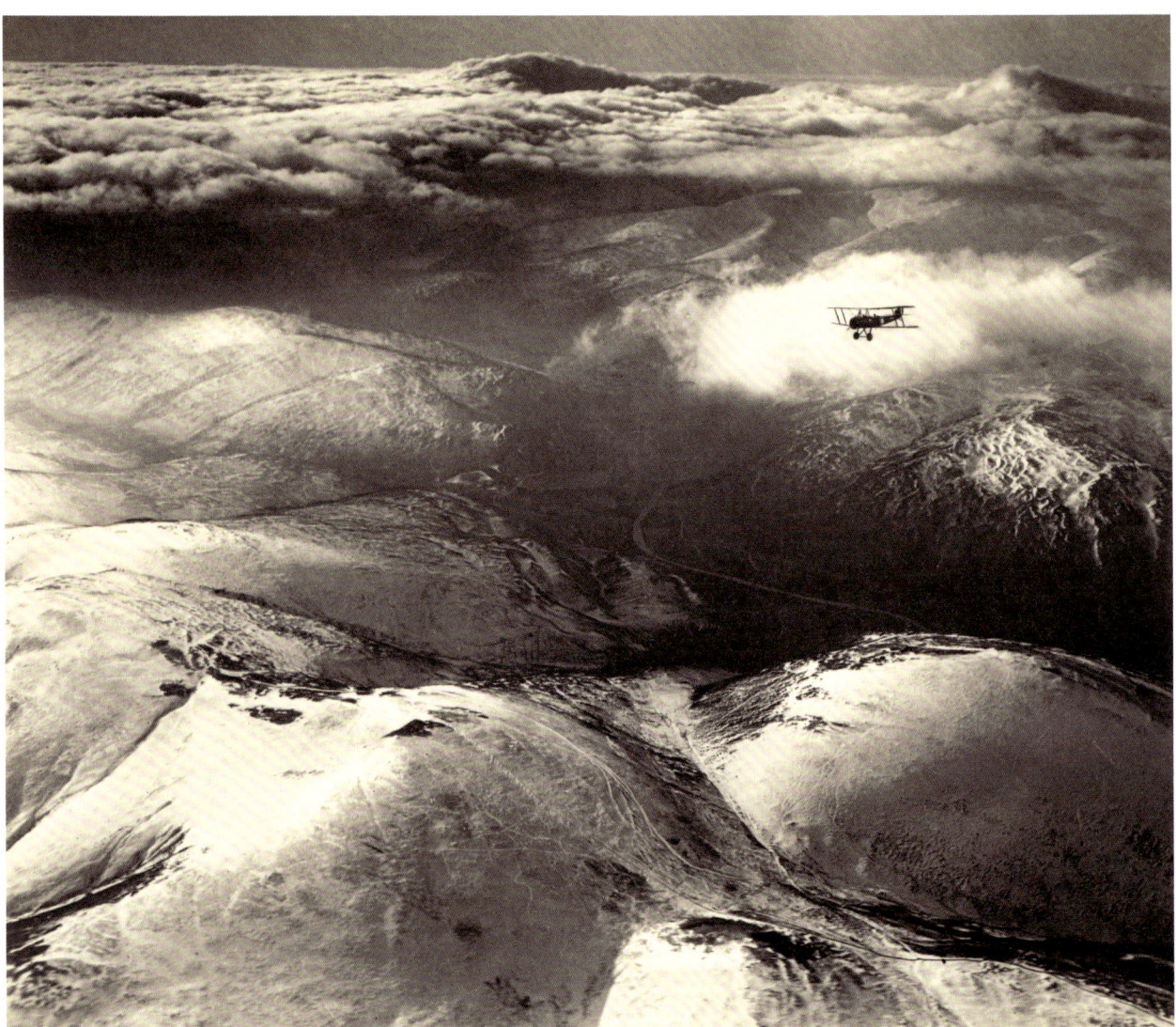

engineering appears in numerous pictures, photographed from a variety of angles and at a range of distances. Its distinctive shape added unrivalled drama to the landscape and allowed Buckham to make a visual connection between the transportation innovations of the previous century and the modern world of aviation that he inhabited.

The same negative of the bridge, looking north towards Fife, was used as the basis of several prints including *The Forth Bridge* (46). To ensure the detail of the bridge's pioneering cantilever design was not lost in the final print, Buckham strengthened the appearances of the trusses with black paint. This negative was also used to produce a Christmas card for RAF Turnhouse in 1918 (54). Showing an aeroplane flying towards the Forth Bridge, this is probably one of the first composite photographs Buckham created.

↑
56. *Morning over the Moorfoots*, *c.*1920, gelatin silver print, **38.3 × 46 cm.** National Galleries of Scotland. Purchased with Art Fund support, 2008

→
57. *Sunset over the Pentland Range*, *c.*1920, gelatin silver print, **46 × 38 cm.** National Galleries of Scotland. Purchased with Art Fund support, 2008

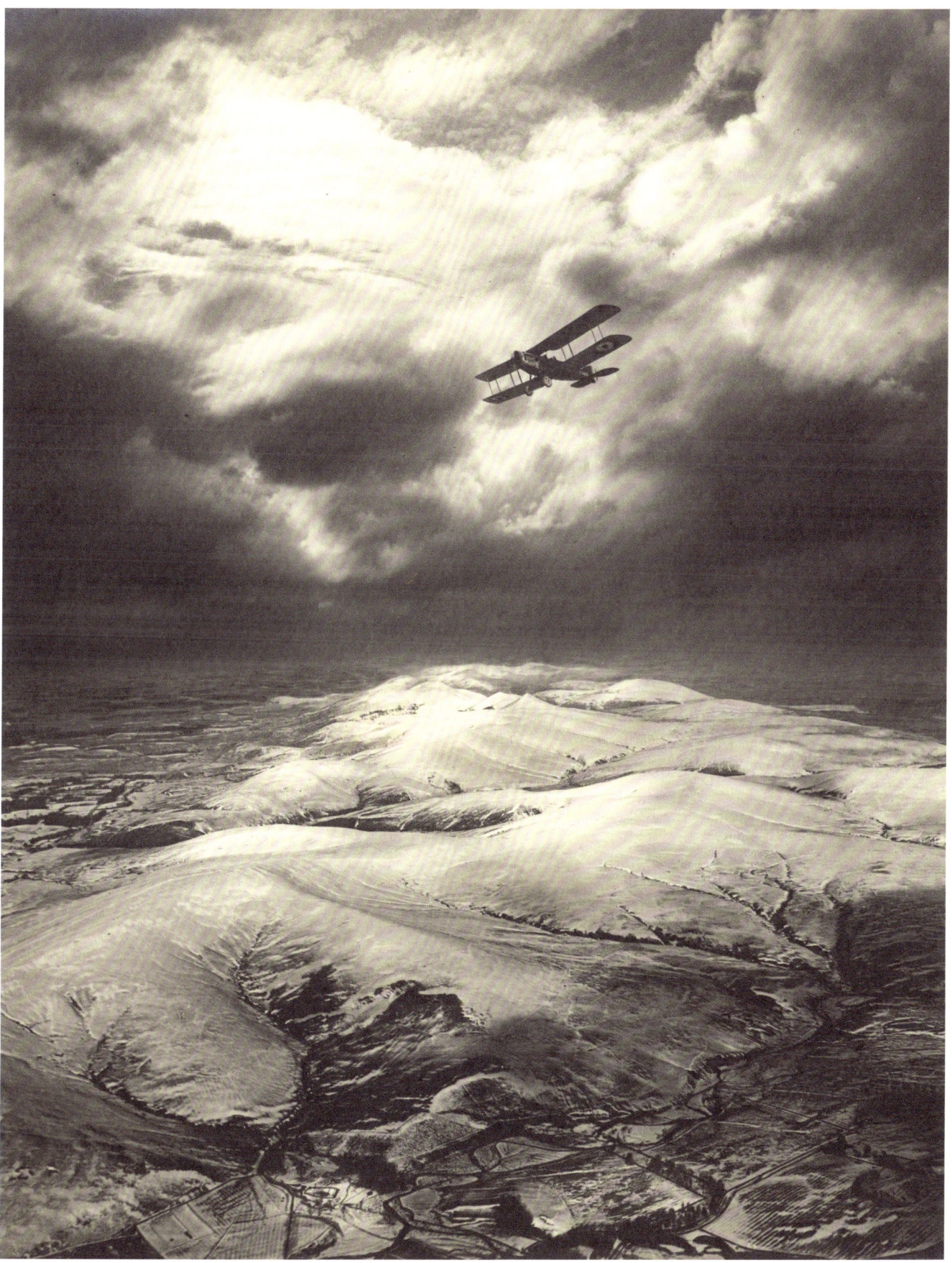

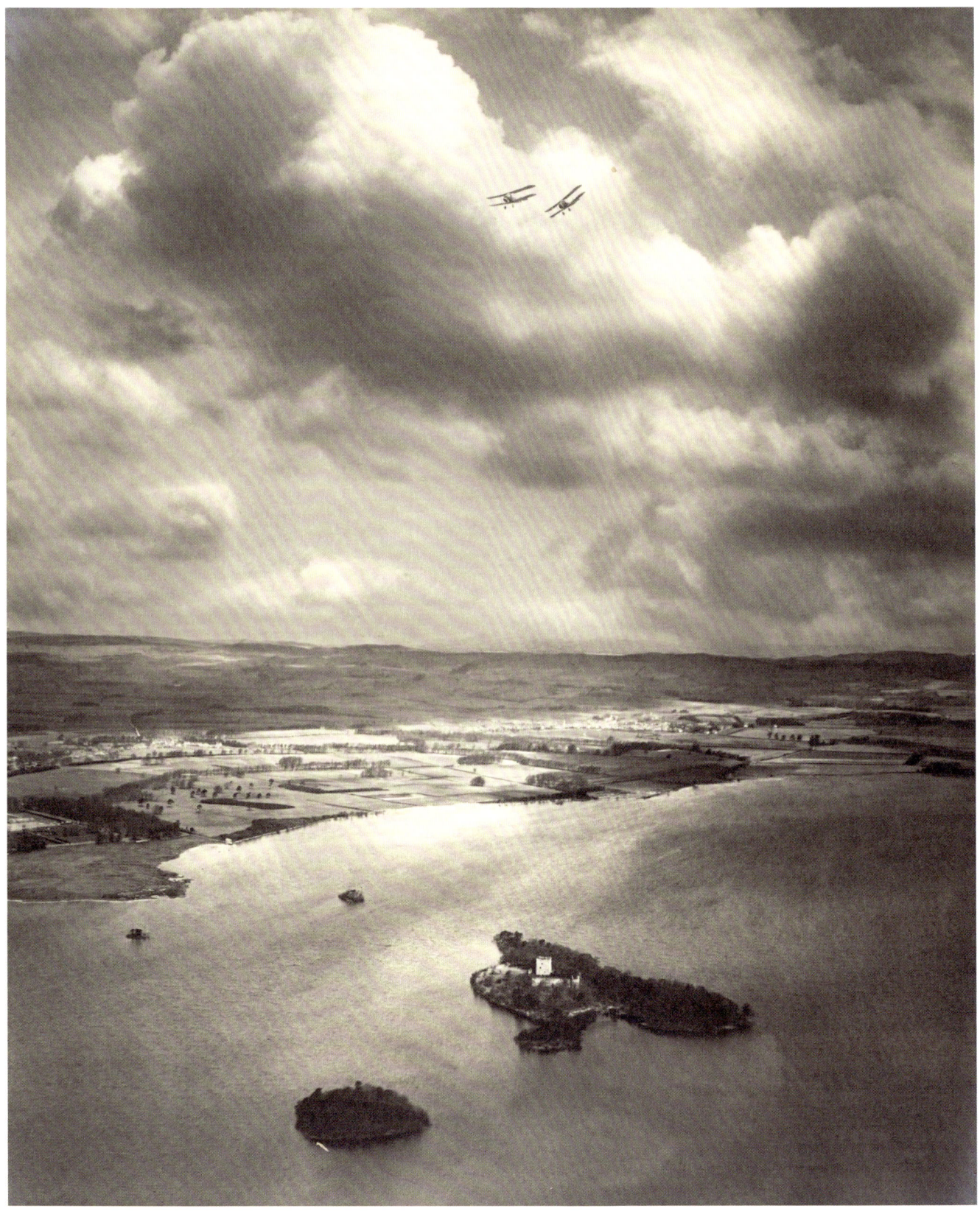

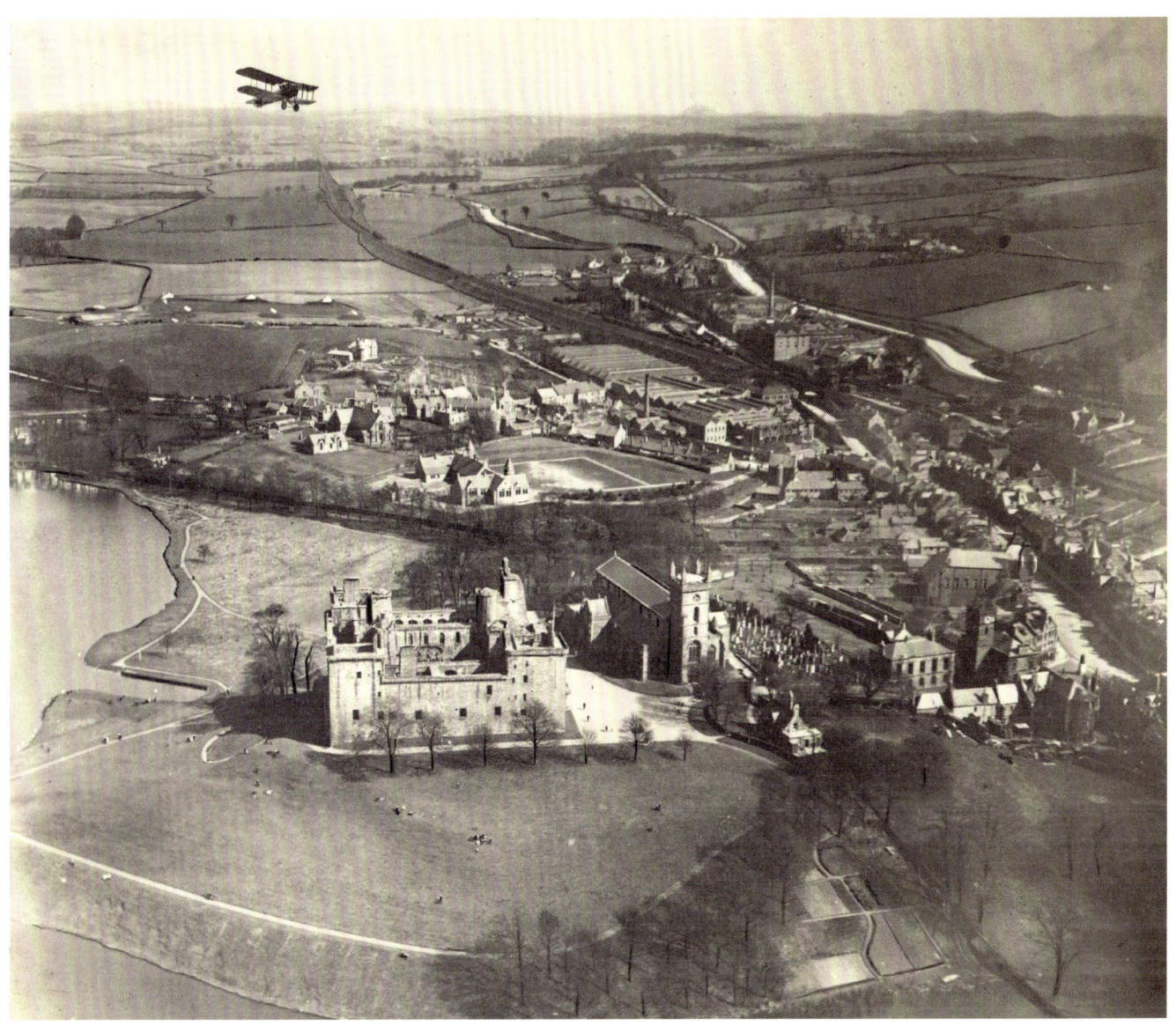

←
58. *Castle Island, Loch Leven (Where Mary, Queen of Scots, was Imprisoned),* *c.*1920, gelatin silver print, 46 × 38.2 cm. National Galleries of Scotland. Purchased with Art Fund support, 2008

↑
59. *Linlithgow Palace,* *c.*1920, gelatin silver print, 38.1 × 45.6 cm. Collection of Richard and John Buckham

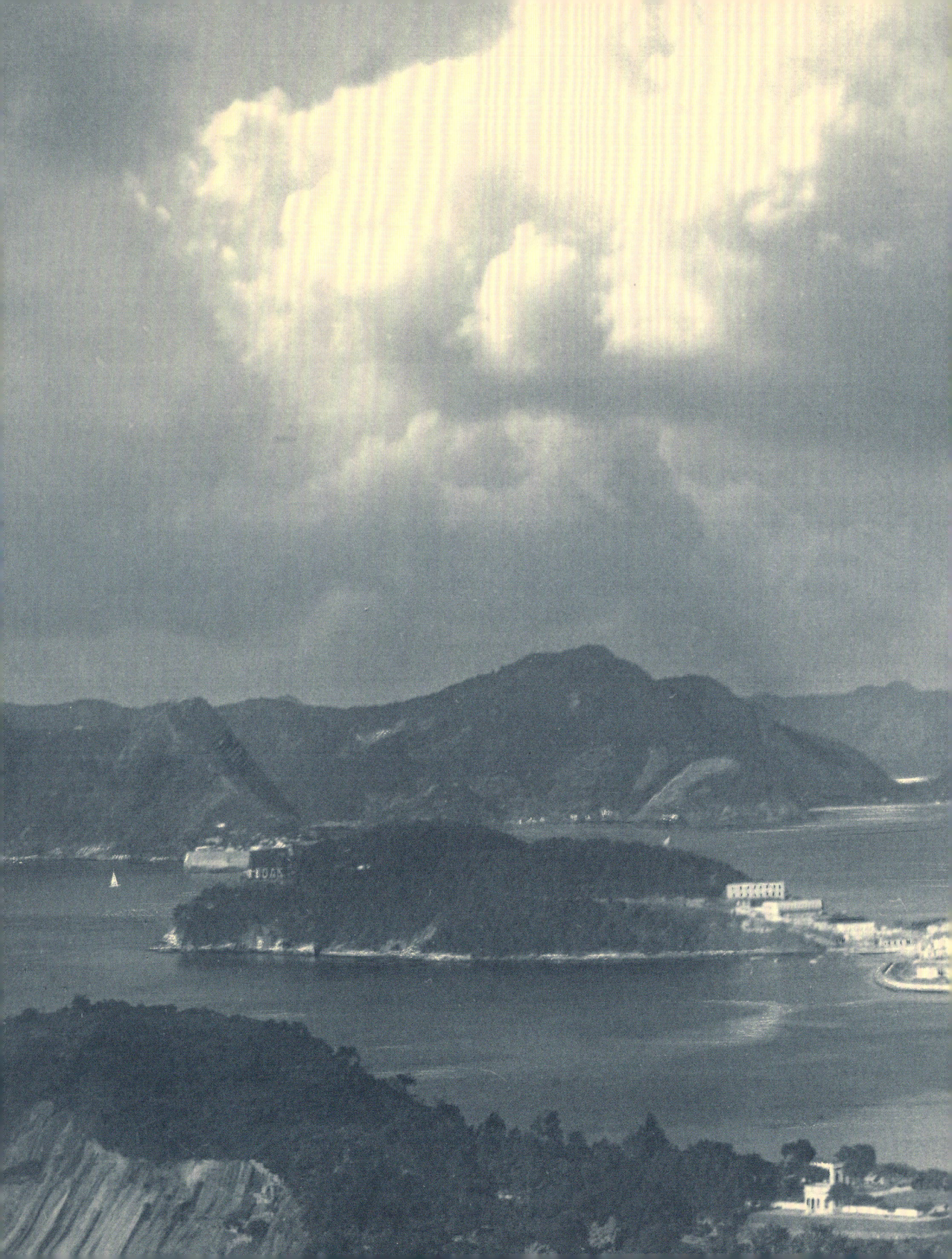

In the
Americas

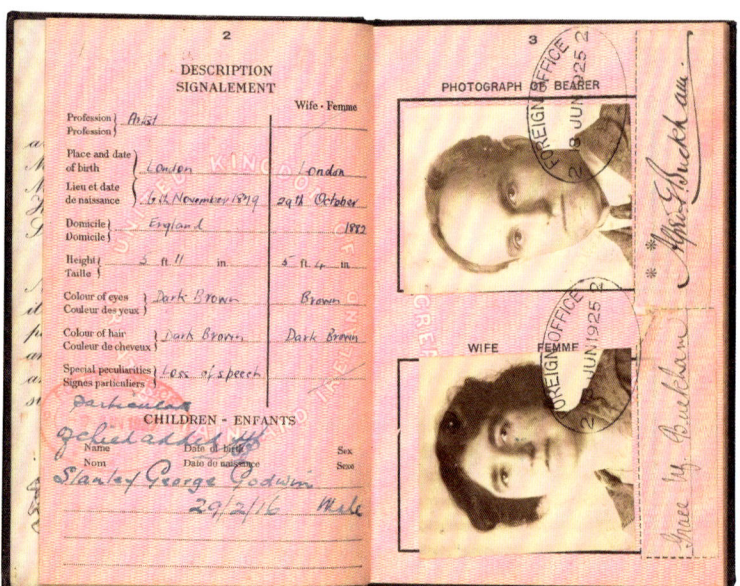

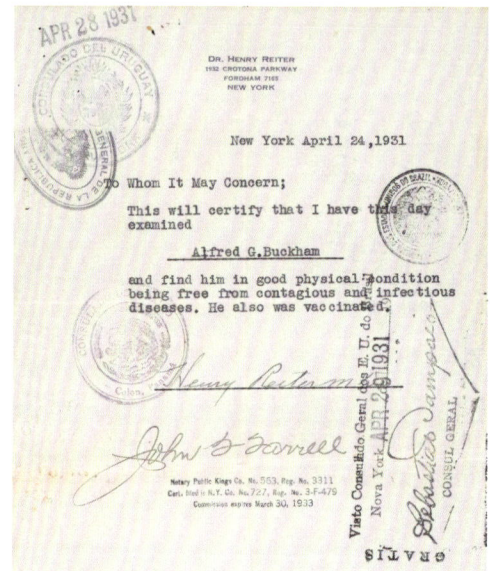

IN 1931 BUCKHAM EMBARKED on his greatest adventure. He was commissioned by the high-end American magazine *Fortune* 'to take aerial photographs anywhere in America'.[1] The result was an epic aerial tour of South America taking fifteen weeks and covering an astonishing, world-record-breaking 19,000 miles.[2]

It was the golden age of travel. Aspirational publications such as *Fortune* and the *National Geographic Magazine* were commissioning photographers to explore the world. Buckham had the winning combination of captivating images and a flair for describing his escapades. Such was the interest in his journey that the *Morning Post* invited him to write an account of his adventure, which they serialised in three parts over the winter of 1933–34. The newspaper's editor gave this introduction: 'These articles ... provide exciting reading and are, moreover – though quite unconsciously so – a record of cheerful pluck in the face of often desperate difficulties'.[3]

With Buckham's adventure predating commercial transatlantic flights, he began his journey by sailing to New York. He described the accommodation on board in a letter to his son Stanley:

I am sleeping in a top berth which I have to climb to. It is quite an acrobatic performance, especially since the steward, who heard I had been in the Navy, took the berth ladder away. I suppose he thought it an insult to a Naval man to give him a ladder to climb into his bed.[4]

Despite the acrobatics, Buckham arrived safely in America in April 1931 and secured the necessary documentation to continue his travels:

↖
60. Alfred Buckham's passport, 1926, 15 × 19.5 cm. Collection of Richard and John Buckham

↑
61. Health certificate issued in New York, 24 April 1931, 17.5 × 15 cm. Collection of Richard and John Buckham

→
62. *New York, across the Hudson River*, 1931, gelatin silver print, 46 × 38 cm. Collection of Richard and John Buckham

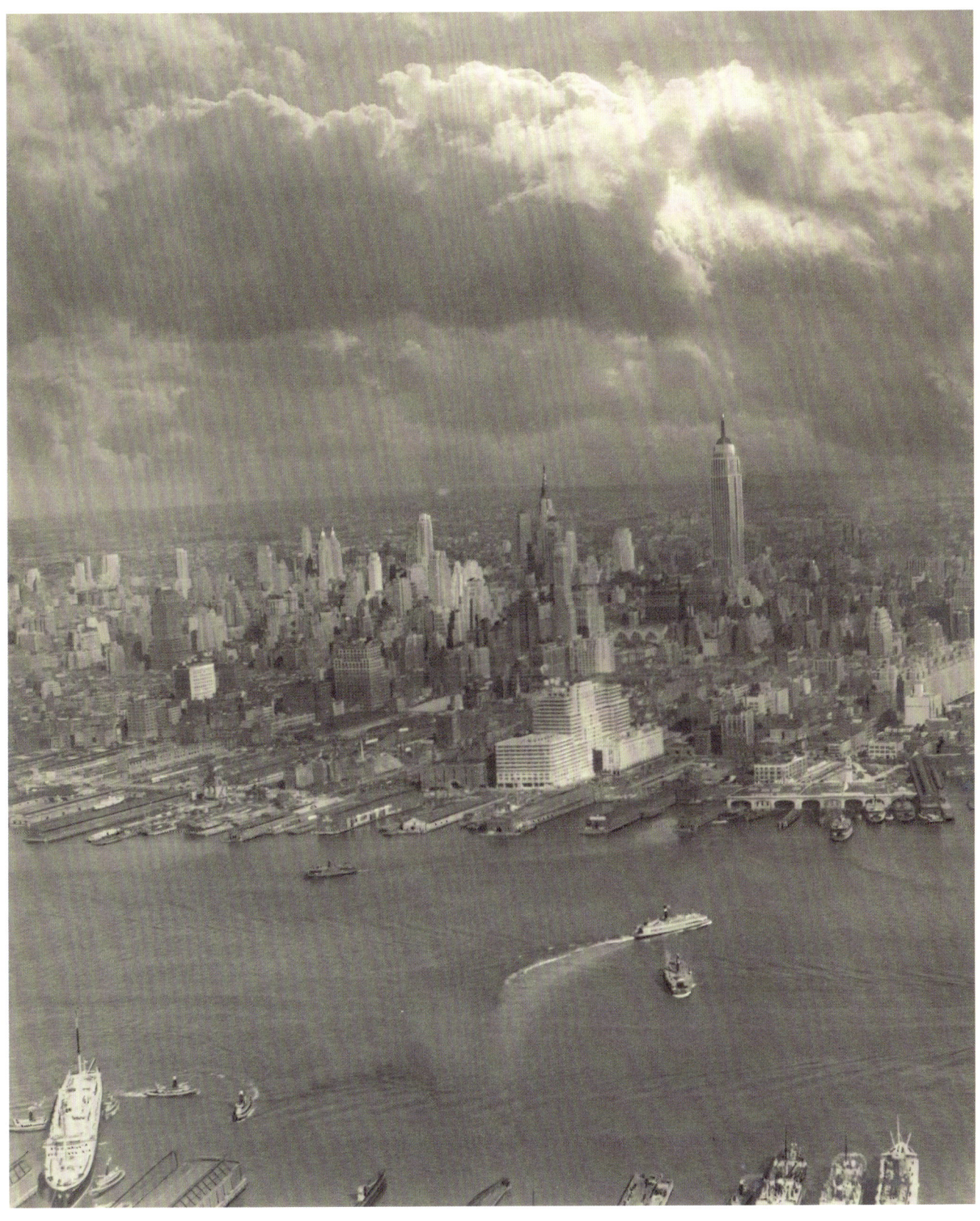

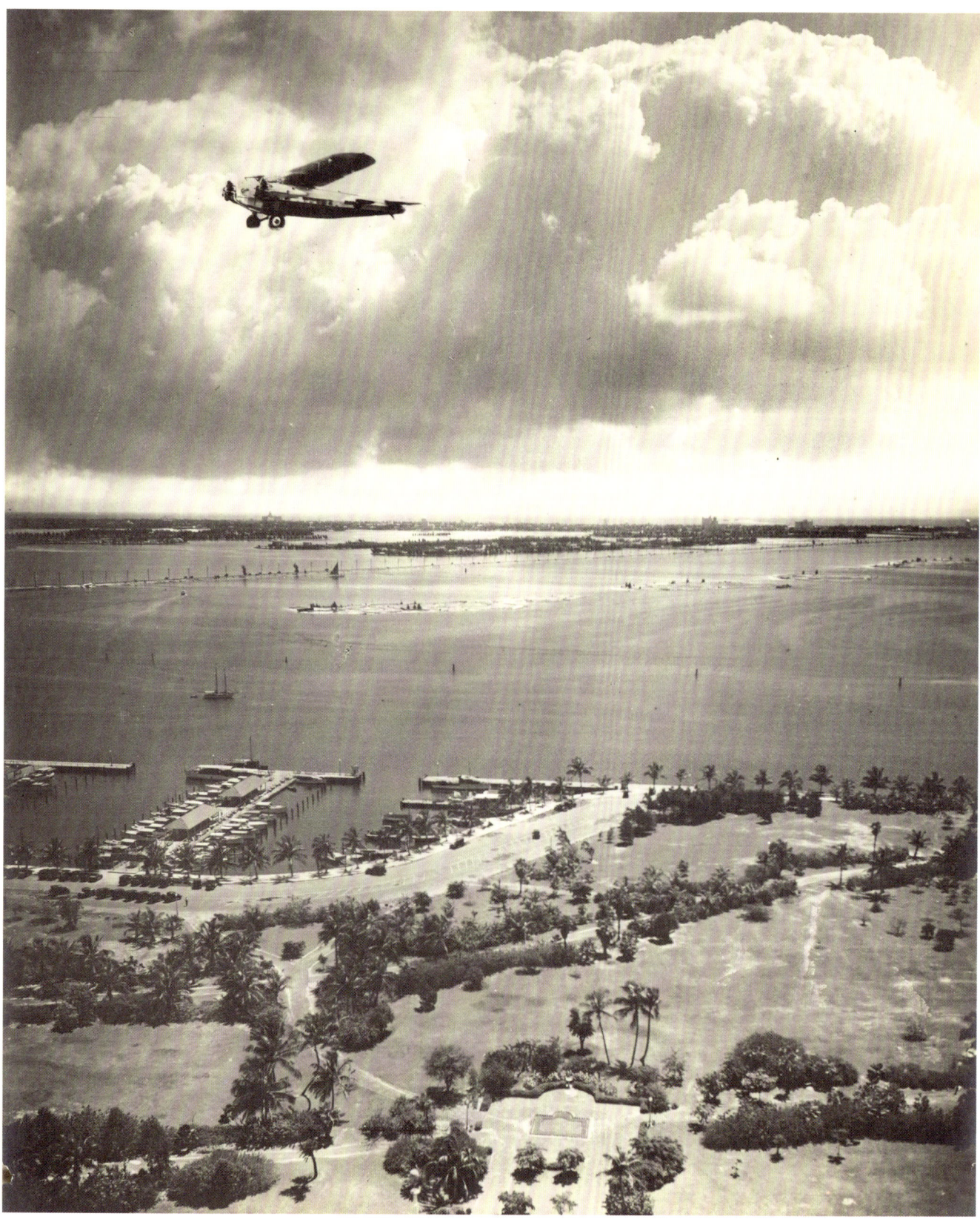

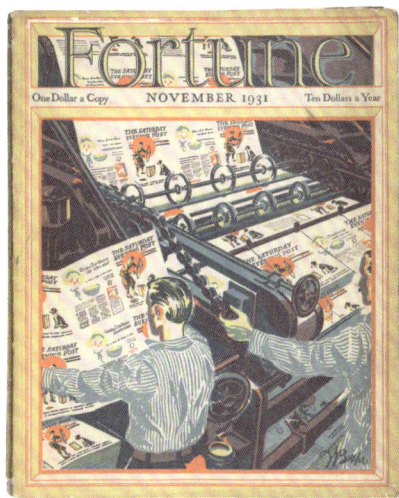
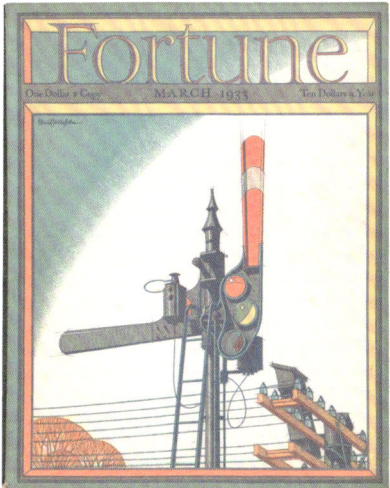
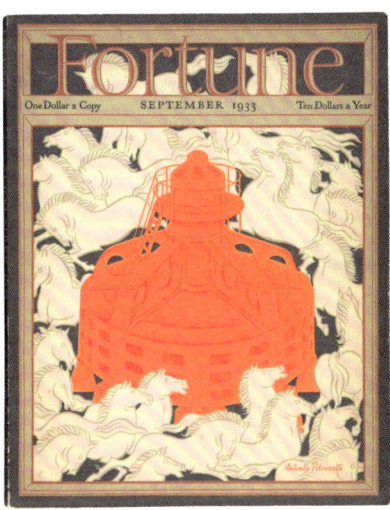

63. *Miami, Florida*, 1931, gelatin silver print, 50.5 × 40.5 cm. Collection of Richard and John Buckham

64. *Fortune*, November 1931, March 1933 and September 1933, each 35 × 29 cm. Collection of Richard and John Buckham

I carried a medical certificate supplied by a remarkably prescient doctor, who, for the inadequate sum of ten dollars, was able to affirm, without seeing me, that I had been vaccinated within the last three months and was entirely free of a whole list of terrible diseases. Surely the most respectable among South American Republics could not deny facilities to such a well certified aerial photographer.[5]

Before leaving New York, Buckham took the opportunity to photograph the newly completed Empire State Building (62). To ensure it appeared suitably majestic on the New York skyline, he scratched back to the white paper to emphasise where the light hit the highest part of the skyscraper. Leaving America in a hired aeroplane via the mud flats of Georgia and sunny Florida, he headed over the Gulf of Mexico to Cuba, encountering his first whale en route.[6]

The first place on the journey to really capture his interest was the Caribbean island of Saba (66). He made extensive notes about this volcanic land mass in his journal, marvelling at the ingenuity of the Dutch population who made boats in the crater and used ropes to lower them 800 feet to sea level.[7] From there, he flew over British Dominica and the tempestuous Mount Pelée volcano of Martinque, which buried 30,000 nearby inhabitants in 1902.[8]

Following the path of the Amazon, Buckham's journey continued in a 'flying boat' (67). These aircraft, such as the Pan-American Air Mail

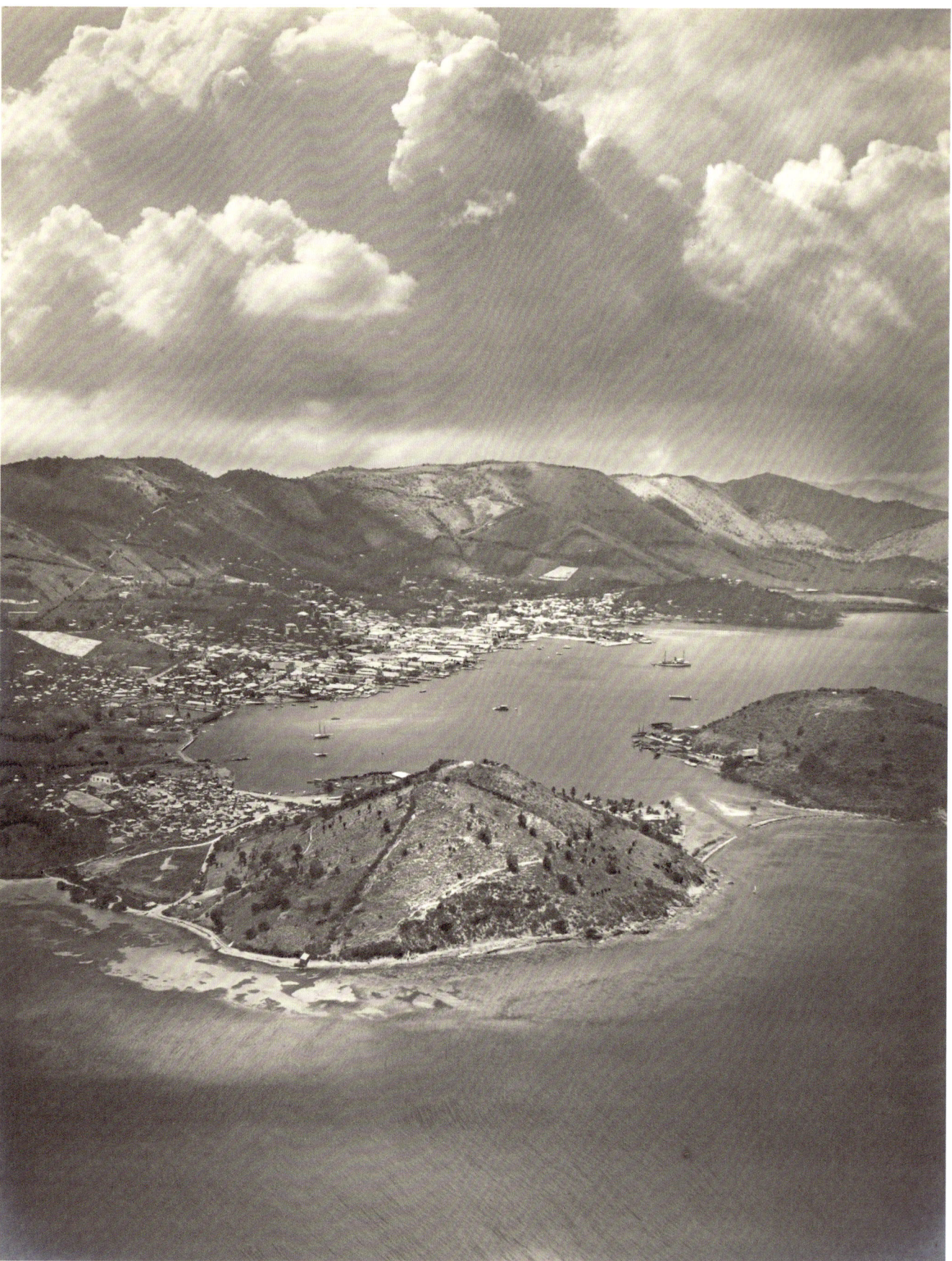

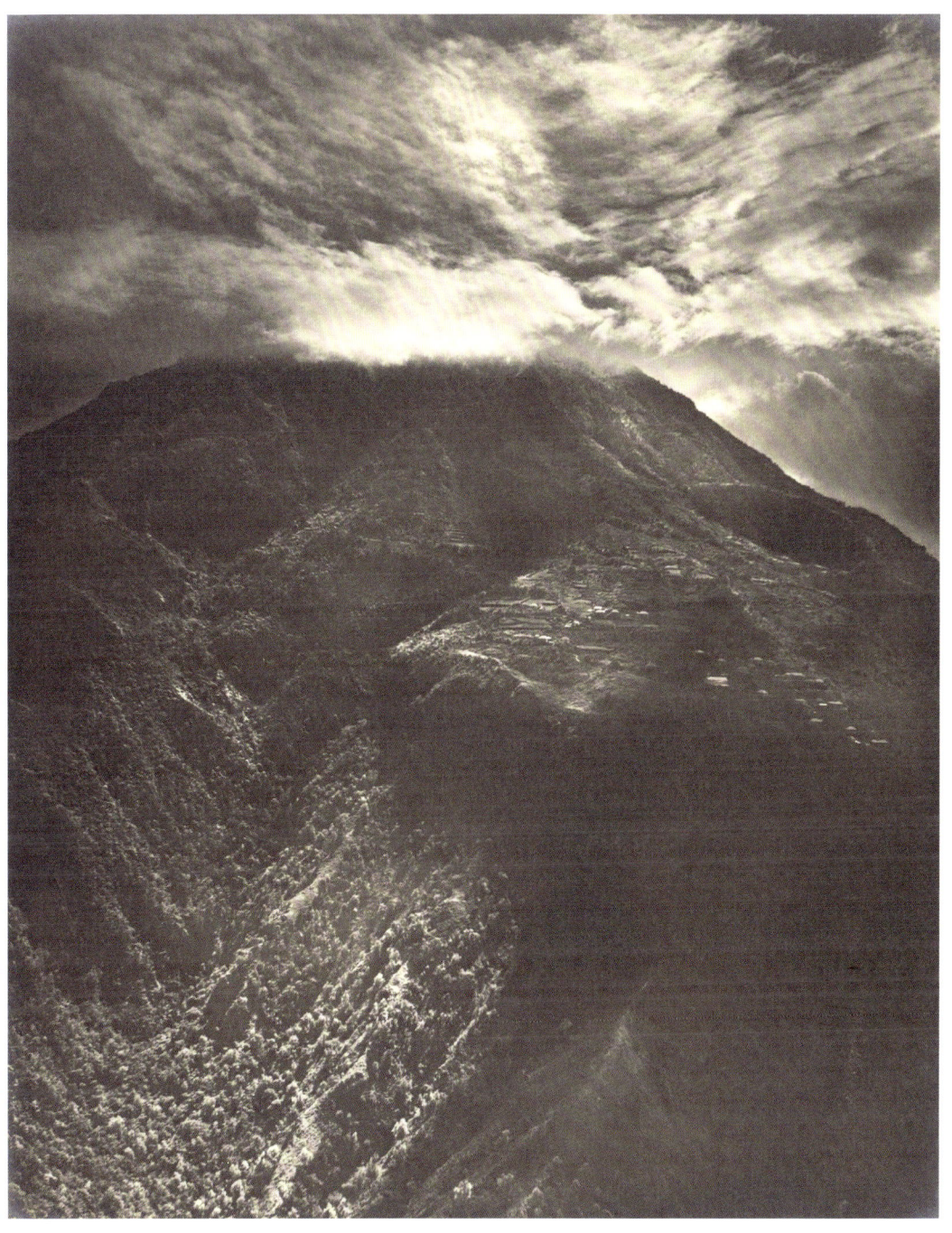

←
65. *St Thomas. Virgin Islands, 'The Pirate's Harbour'*, 1931, gelatin silver print, 50.8 × 40.5 cm. Collection of Richard and John Buckham

↑
66. *The Mountain Shipyard of Saba*, 1931, gelatin silver print, 51 × 40.8 cm. Collection of Richard and John Buckham

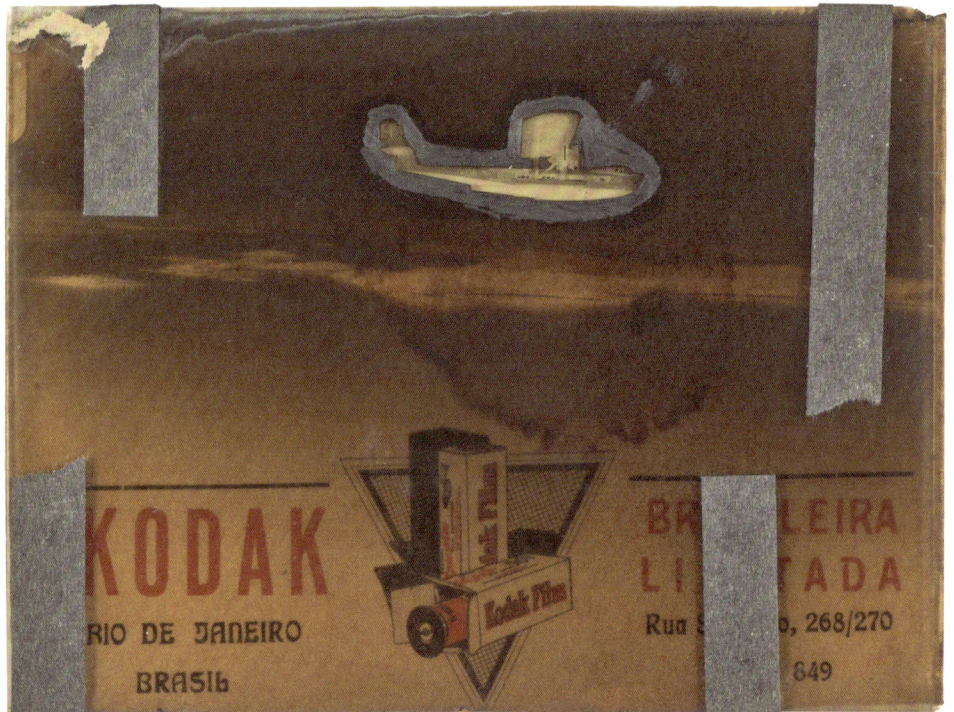

seaplane photographed, were designed to be flown low on the cushion of
air that sits just above the surface of the water.[9] Buckham's photographs
of South America were created with less manipulation in the darkroom
than his earlier images, but he was still relying on his usual method to add
in aeroplanes when he felt they were required to recount his expedition.

The Amazon led him to Brazil and Argentina, where he was forced to
navigate the full force of South American bureaucracy. Laid down with
the flu in Buenos Aires, Buckham relied on local knowledge to secure the
necessary permissions to fly:

*Fortunately, that intrepid fellow Eduardo Bradley [1887–1951, an
Argentinian pilot] – the first man to cross the Andes in a balloon and who
walks despite a broken back sustained in his last aerial adventure – carried
out the negotiations. Unauthorised aeroplanes flying over the city were
liable to be shot down, because South American revolutionaries have an
unpleasant habit of conducting preliminary operations from the air.*[10]

Fearing the authorities would change their mind, Buckham raced from
his sickbed to the military aerodrome. This particular flight, however,
was destined to be ill-fated: 'My journey nearly came to an abrupt
conclusion over Buenos Aires, for the door of the cabin aeroplane
through the window of which I leaned to photograph idly swung wide
open as I drew back to change a dark slide. The safety catch

↖
67. *Flying Boat*, 1931, glass
plate negative, 10 × 12.5 cm.
National Galleries of Scotland.
Purchased from Richard and
John Buckham 2019

→
68. *Flying Boat over Sea*,
1931, gelatin silver print,
45.5 × 37.6 cm. National Galleries
of Scotland. Purchased with Art
Fund support, 2008

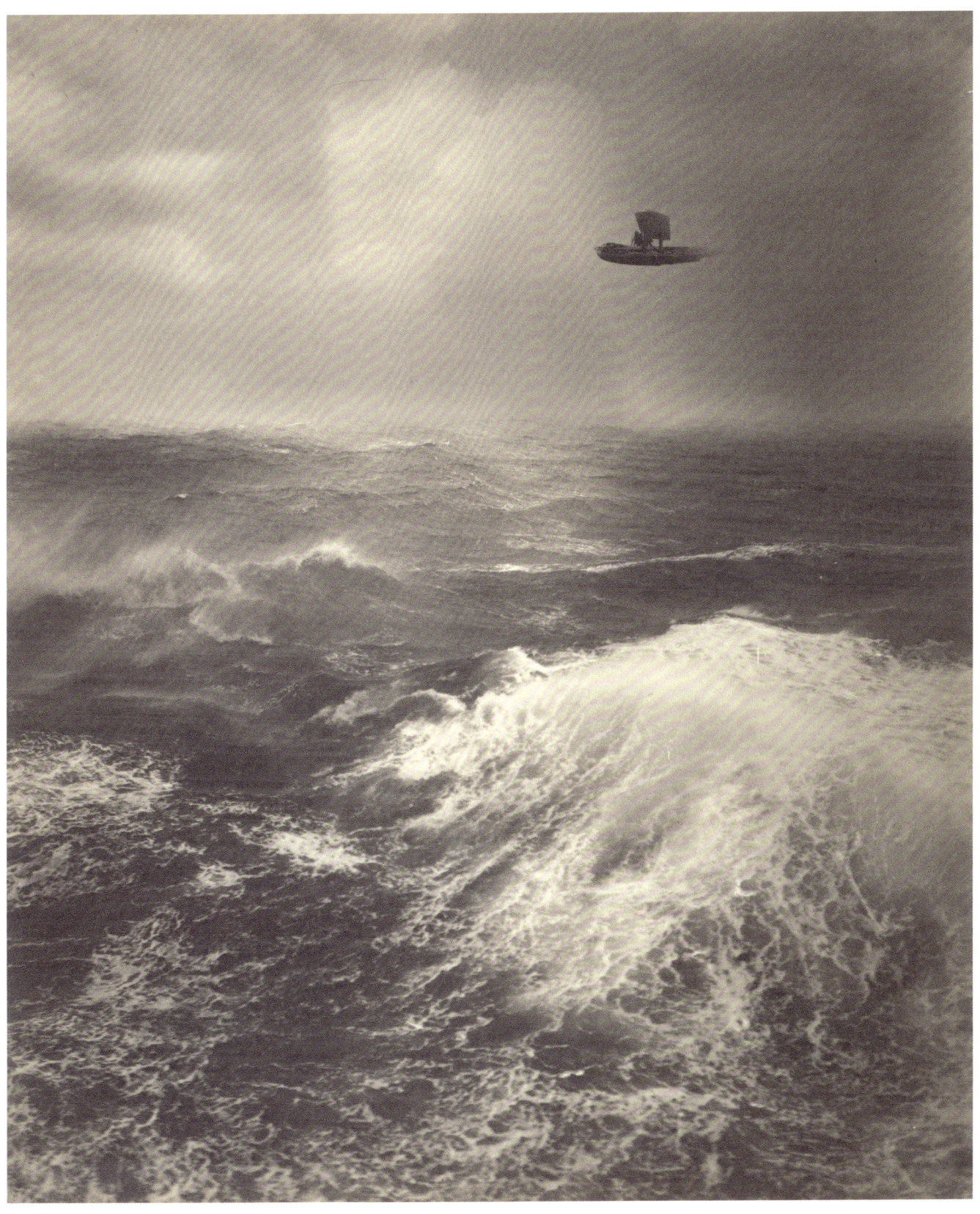

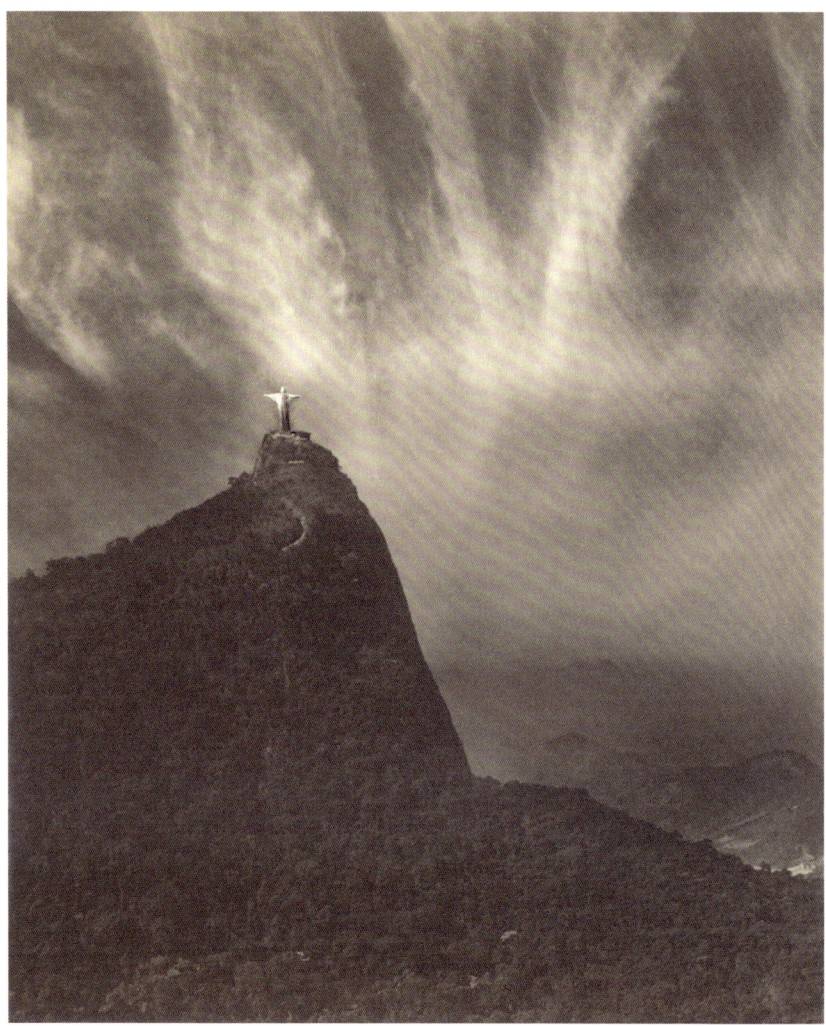

was broken.'[11] To add insult to injury, on landing, his negatives were subject to intense scrutiny, with military personnel demanding to inspect prints of the images before he was permitted to leave the country. This was a pattern that was repeated throughout his journey, with his camera taped up with 'commendable zeal' on arrival in Chile until permission to photograph was granted.[12]

The next challenge was to cross the Andes (73). Never one to be fazed, Buckham took a pragmatic approach to the dangers of flying at such high altitude with his disability:

Then for the first time in my flying experience, even at greater heights, I began to feel the effects of altitude. Higher we climbed to 18,000ft, my pilot taking oxygen. He passed the tube back to me, but owning to certain physical disabilities I could not use it. Struggling for breath at 19,500ft, I realised that unconsciousness was inevitable, as no attempt could be made

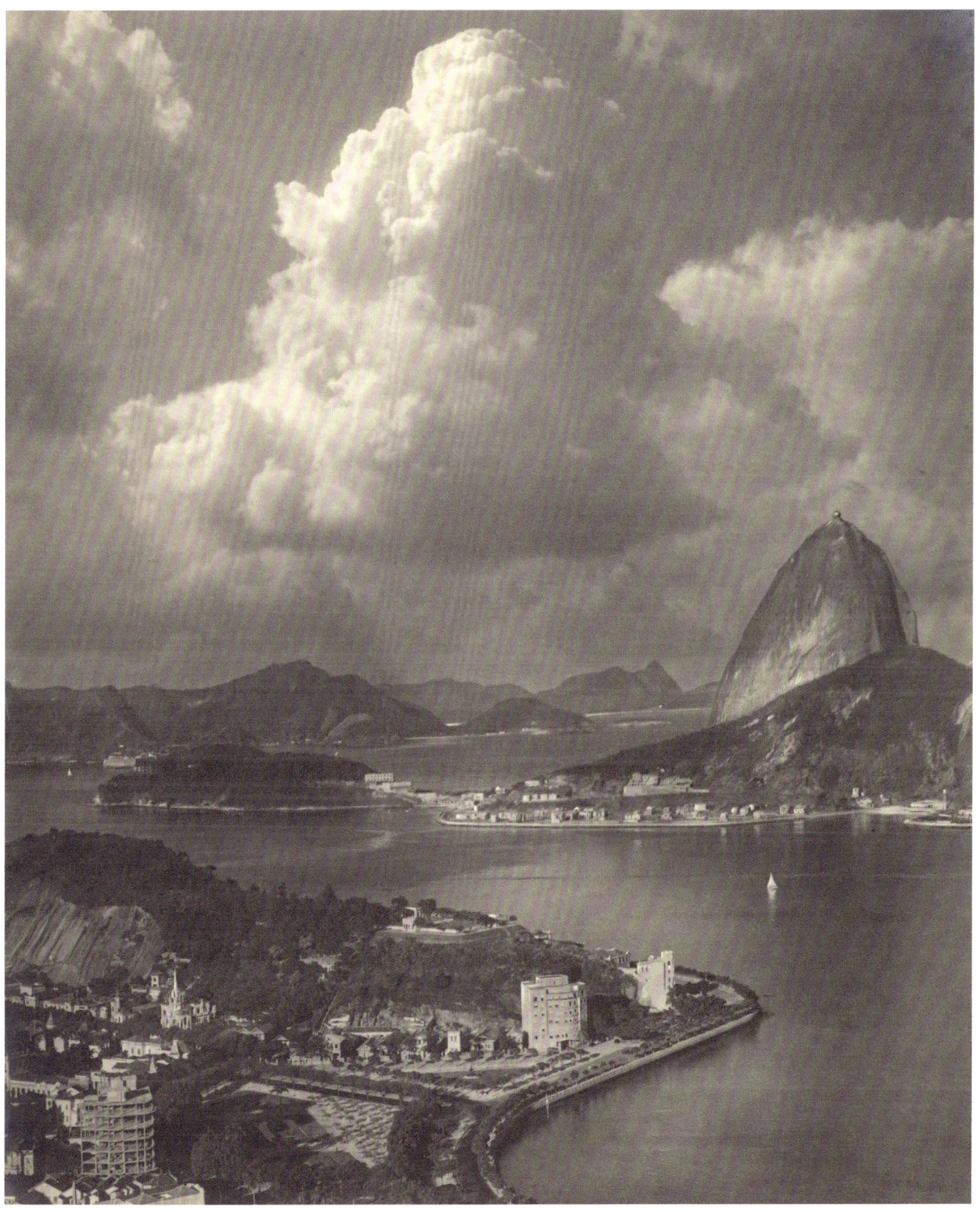

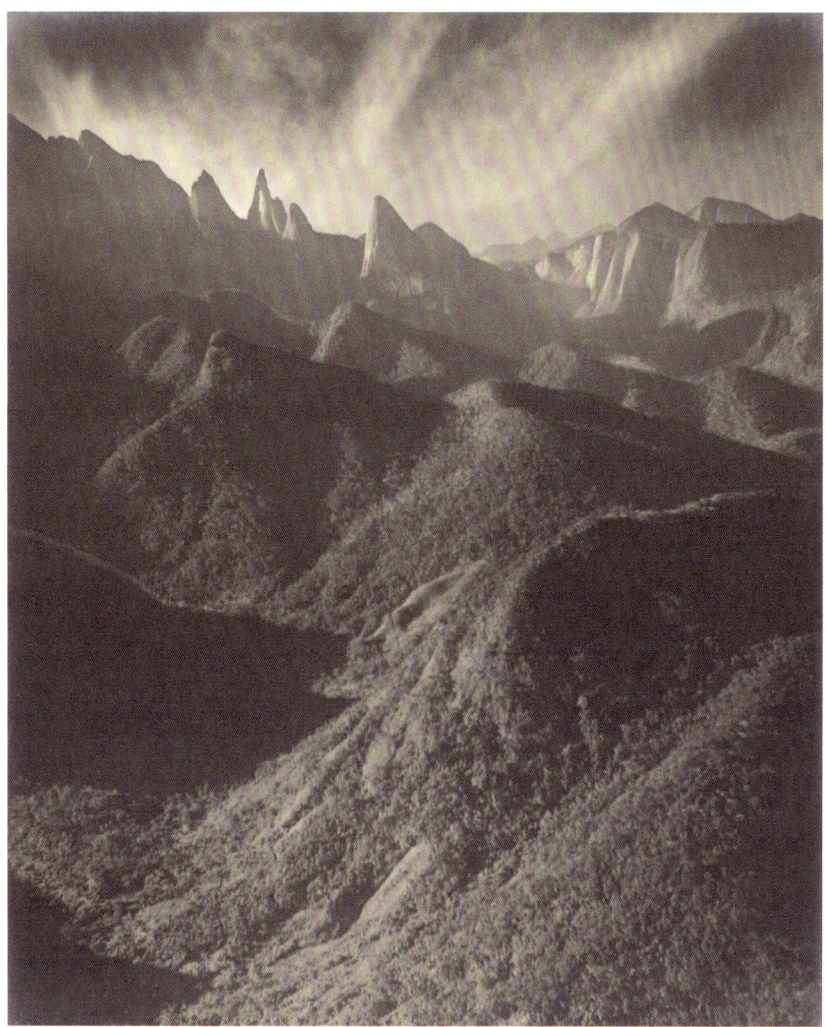

to descend to a lower altitude for at least another fifteen minutes. I passed a note to my companion requesting him to thrust back my head whenever it fell forward; then I settled down in great discomfort, but with perfect confidence that I should survive the remaining minutes before going down.[13]

Having navigated the perils of the snow-capped Andes, and survived, Buckham headed north across the Chilean desert and passed over the remains of ancient civilisations in Peru. In Colombia he was greeted by alligators, which added a little extra excitement to taking off in a seaplane, and was welcomed to Panama by thunderstorms and a deluge of rain.[14] On reaching Lake Nicaragua, the weather cleared and Buckham described the view from between the clouds as sublime (76).[15] His review of the wildlife in Nicaragua was less favourable, and he dedicated a page of his journal to his dislike of rattlesnakes, which he seemed to fear more than performing loop the loops without a safety belt.[16]

↖
71. *'The Fingers of God'. Orgao Mountains* [Serra dos Órgãos], *Brazil*, 1931, gelatin silver print, **46 × 38 cm.** Collection of Richard and John Buckham

↗
72. *The City Hall of Buenos Aires*, 1931, gelatin silver print, **38 × 45.5 cm.** Collection of Richard and John Buckham

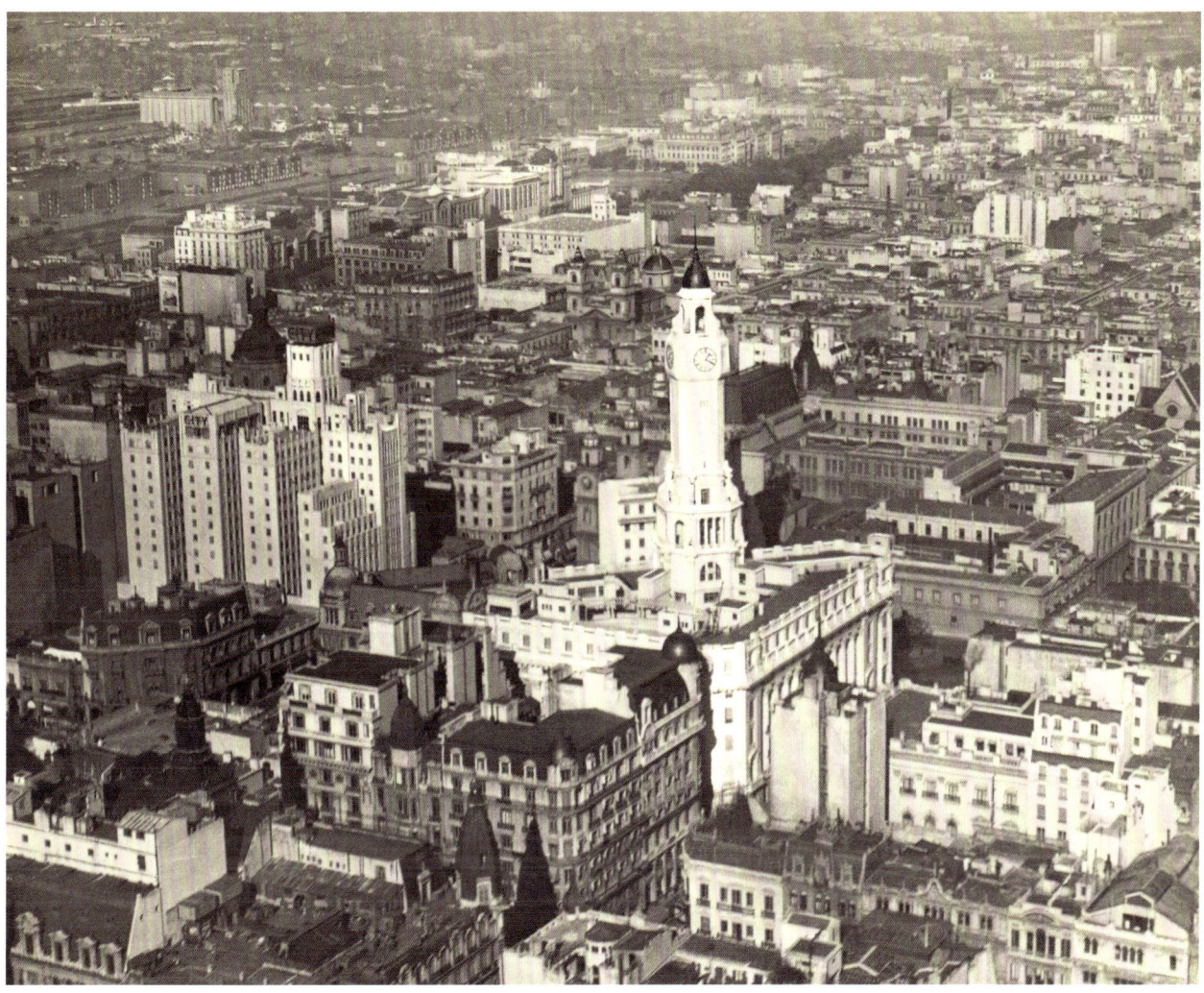

In Central America, Buckham began a game of cat-and-mouse in his mission to photograph an erupting volcano. His first attempt was over the mighty Momotombo volcano in Nicaragua: 'As if resentful of being photographed, the volcano suddenly cast a cloud of choking, sulphurous gas upon us, an unpleasant experience which engendered greater caution in the next approach.'[17] He tried again over Santa María in Guatemala, where a recent eruption had torn away the side of the mountain and buried a village at its base (79).[18]

Moving into Mexico, he was delayed by problems finding a willing pilot. His journey so far had been facilitated by over twenty different pilots, but he struggled to convince anyone to join him on this last hurrah.[19] Eventually, an amateur American pilot decided he was game for an adventure and Buckham again took to the skies.[20] Before resuming his quest to fly inside the mouth of a volcano, he photographed the ancient Pyramid of the Sun and Pyramid of the

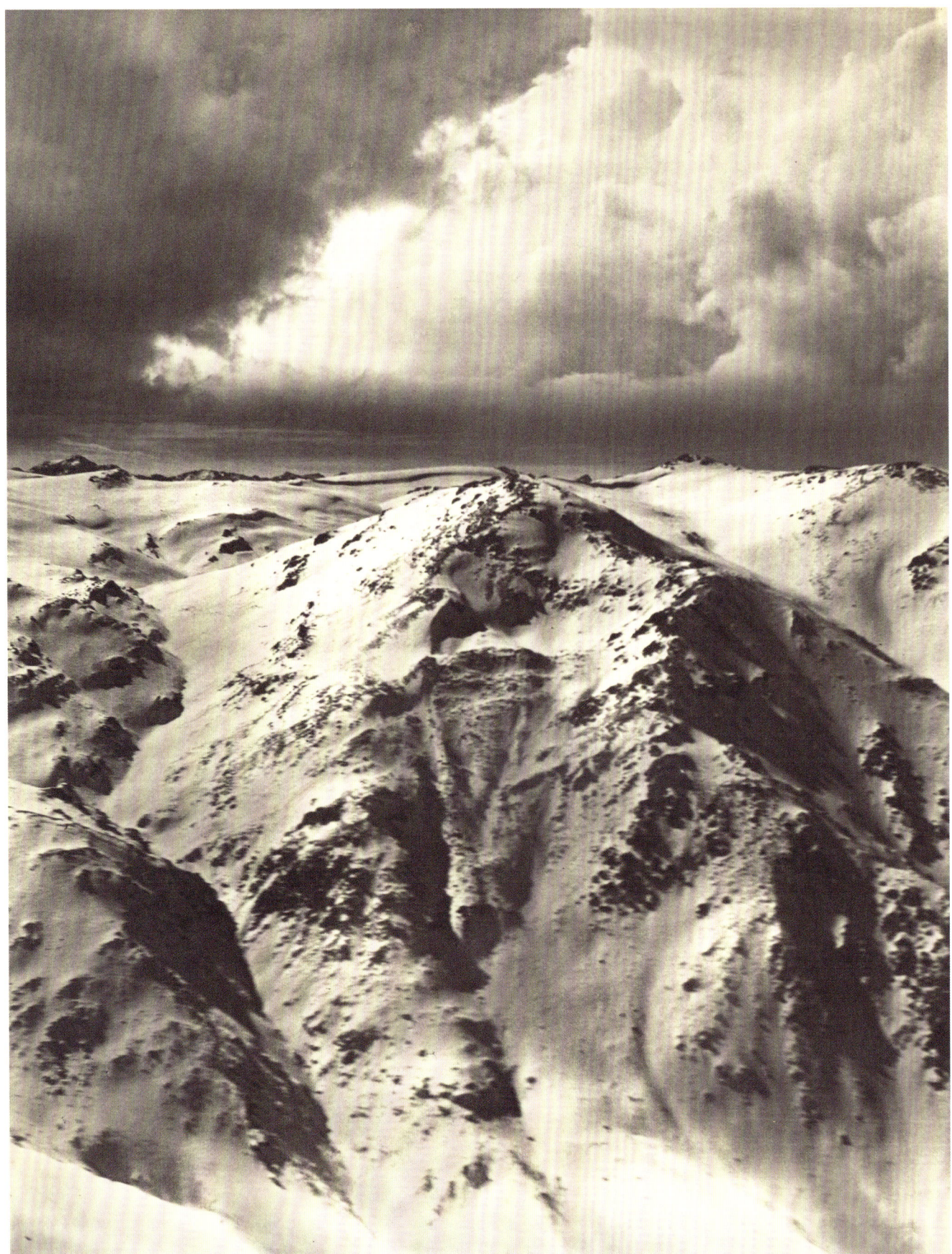

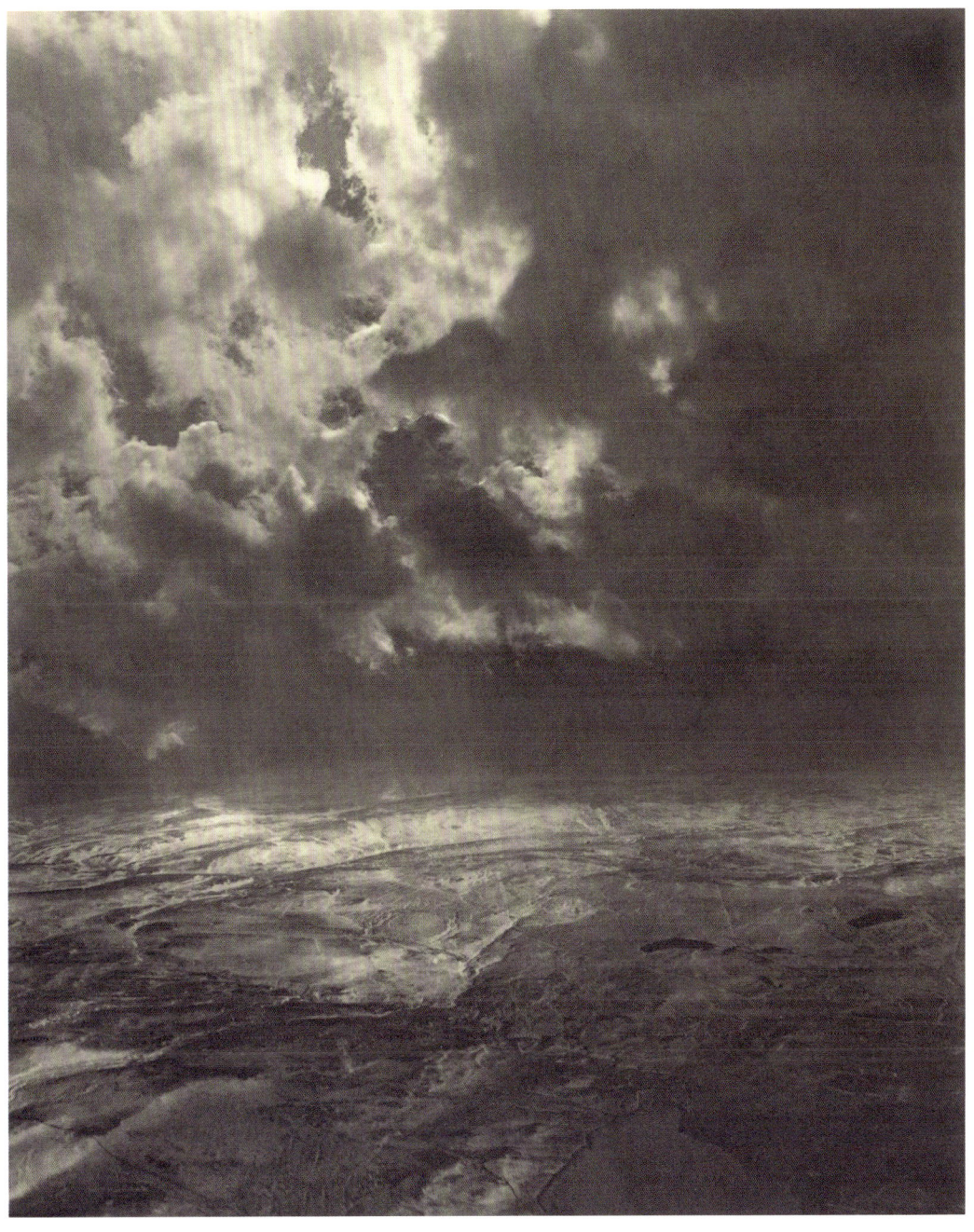

←
73. *Over the Top. The Andes at 19,700 ft*, **1931, gelatin silver print, 50.8 × 41 cm.** Collection of Richard and John Buckham

↑
74. *The Wilderness (Chilean Desert)*, **1931, gelatin silver print, 45.8 × 38.2 cm.** National Galleries of Scotland. Purchased with Art Fund support, 2008

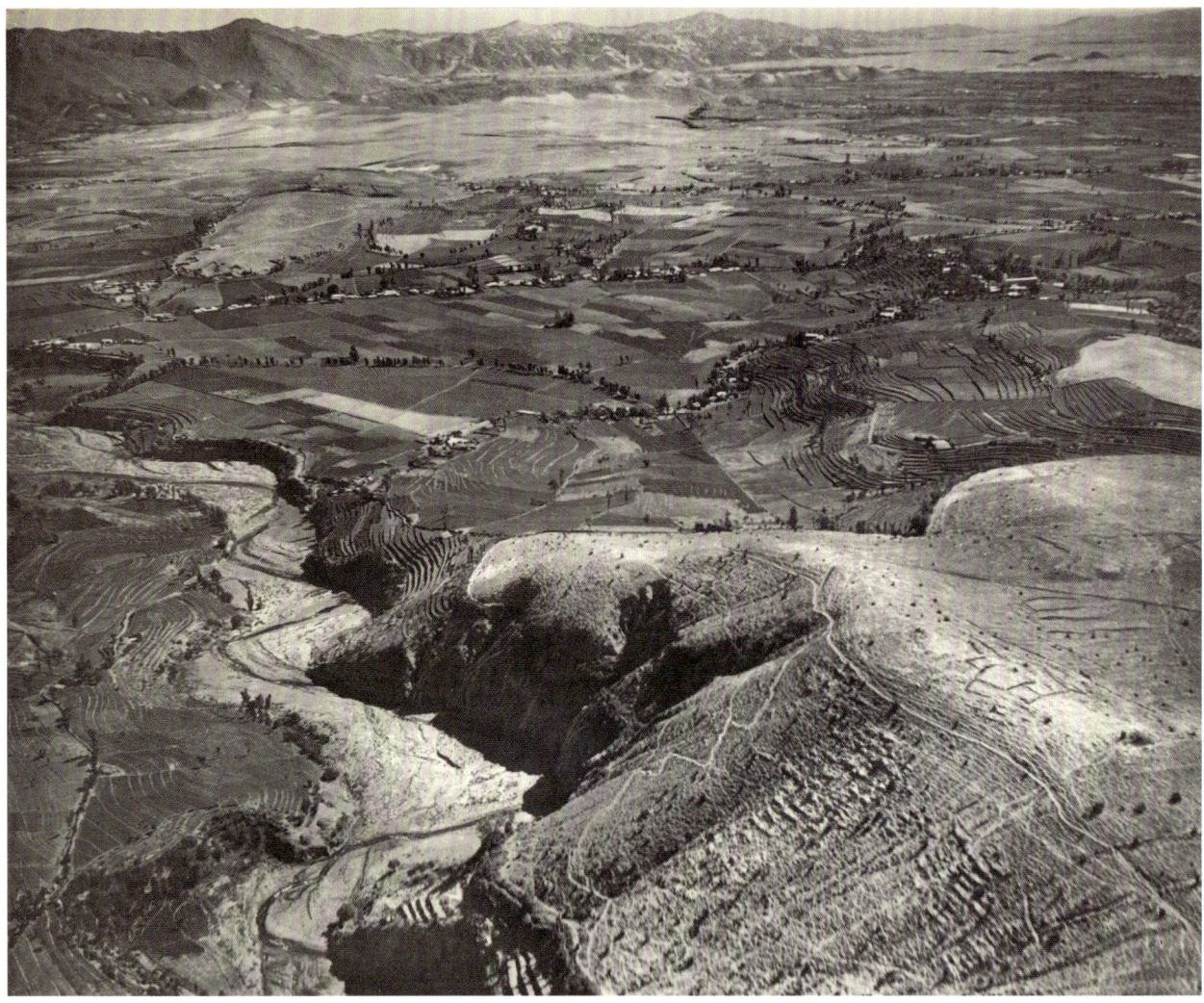

Moon at Teotihuacan (78). As with many of the photographs he made in South America, he attached a label with detailed notes to the mount. Of particular interest was that the Pyramid of the Sun had a footprint only 60 feet smaller than the Great Pyramid of Giza in Egypt.

His sights set on Popocatépetl, a monumental volcano visible from Mexico City, Buckham and his plucky pilot waited several days for the perfect weather conditions to approach the crater. At last they came, with the wake of a strong wind allowing them to pass right across the crater at 18,500 feet.[21]

The pilot indicated his willingness to fly inside the crater, and with this idea in view we came up against the wind again and passed over the lip with about twenty feet to spare. Almost at once the aeroplane dropped about 200ft, being carried down apparently by a current of cold air which,

↑
75. *Peru. Remains of the Pre-Inca Civilisation and Irrigation Ditches. Foothills of the Andes*, 1931, gelatin silver print, 40.8 × 50.8 cm. Collection of Richard and John Buckham

→
76. *Lake Nicaragua*, 1931, gelatin silver print, 50.8 × 41 cm. Collection of Richard and John Buckham

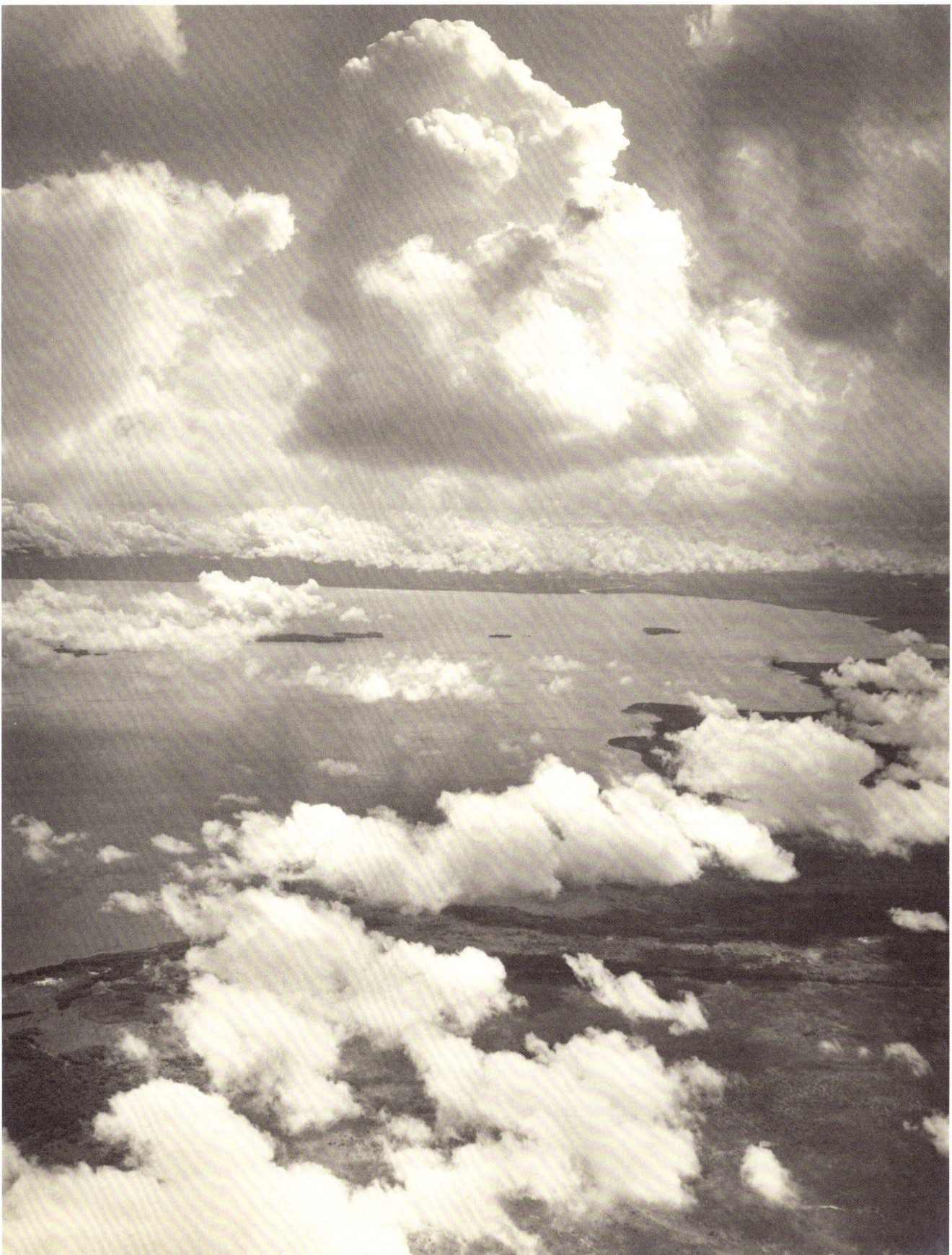

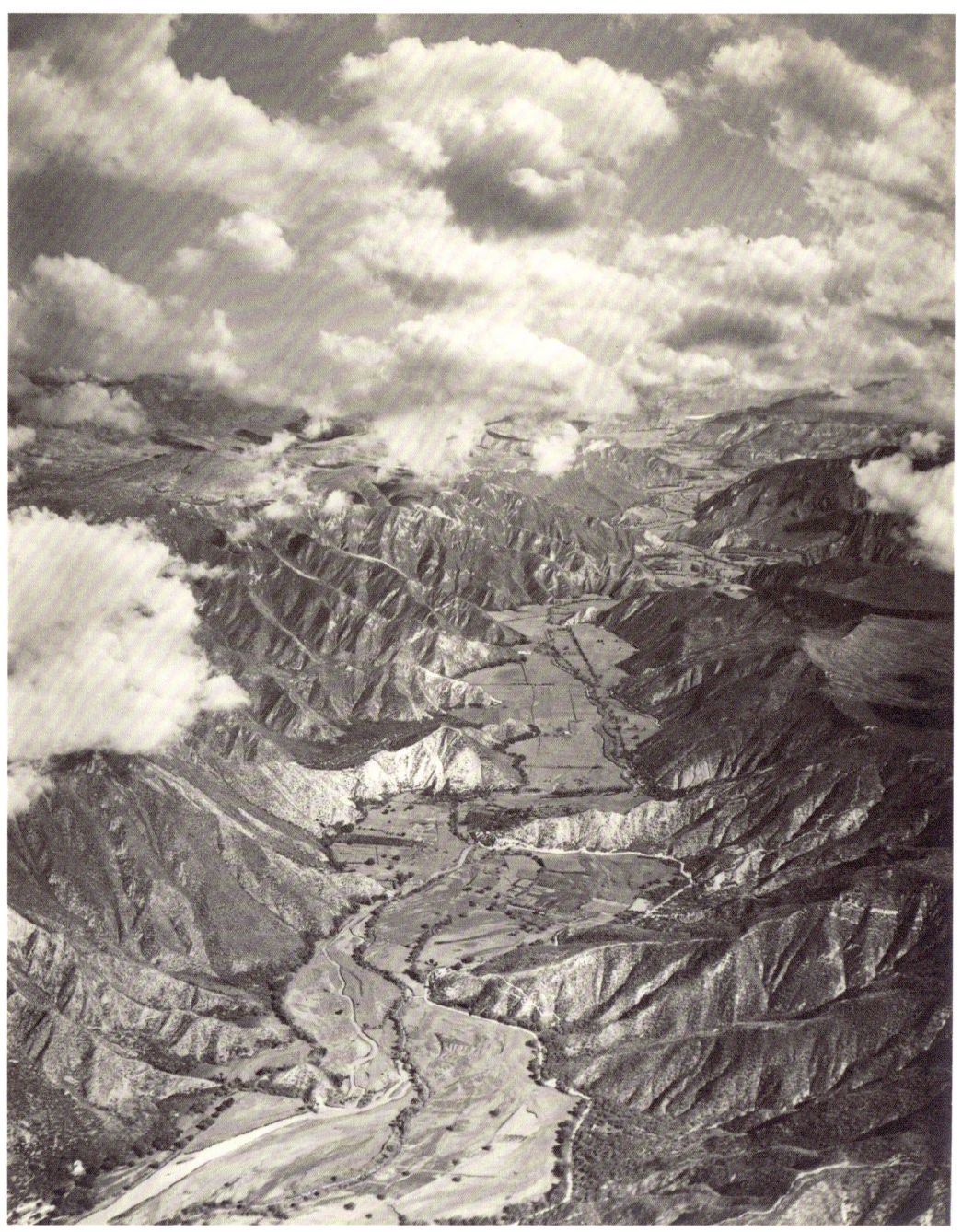

↑
77. *The Mountain Ranges between Tampico and Mexico City*, 1931, gelatin silver print, 50.8 × 40.7 cm. Collection of Richard and John Buckham

→
78. *Mexico. The Pyramids to the Sun and the Moon at Teotihuacan*, 1931, gelatin silver print, 50.7 × 40.6 cm. Collection of Richard and John Buckham

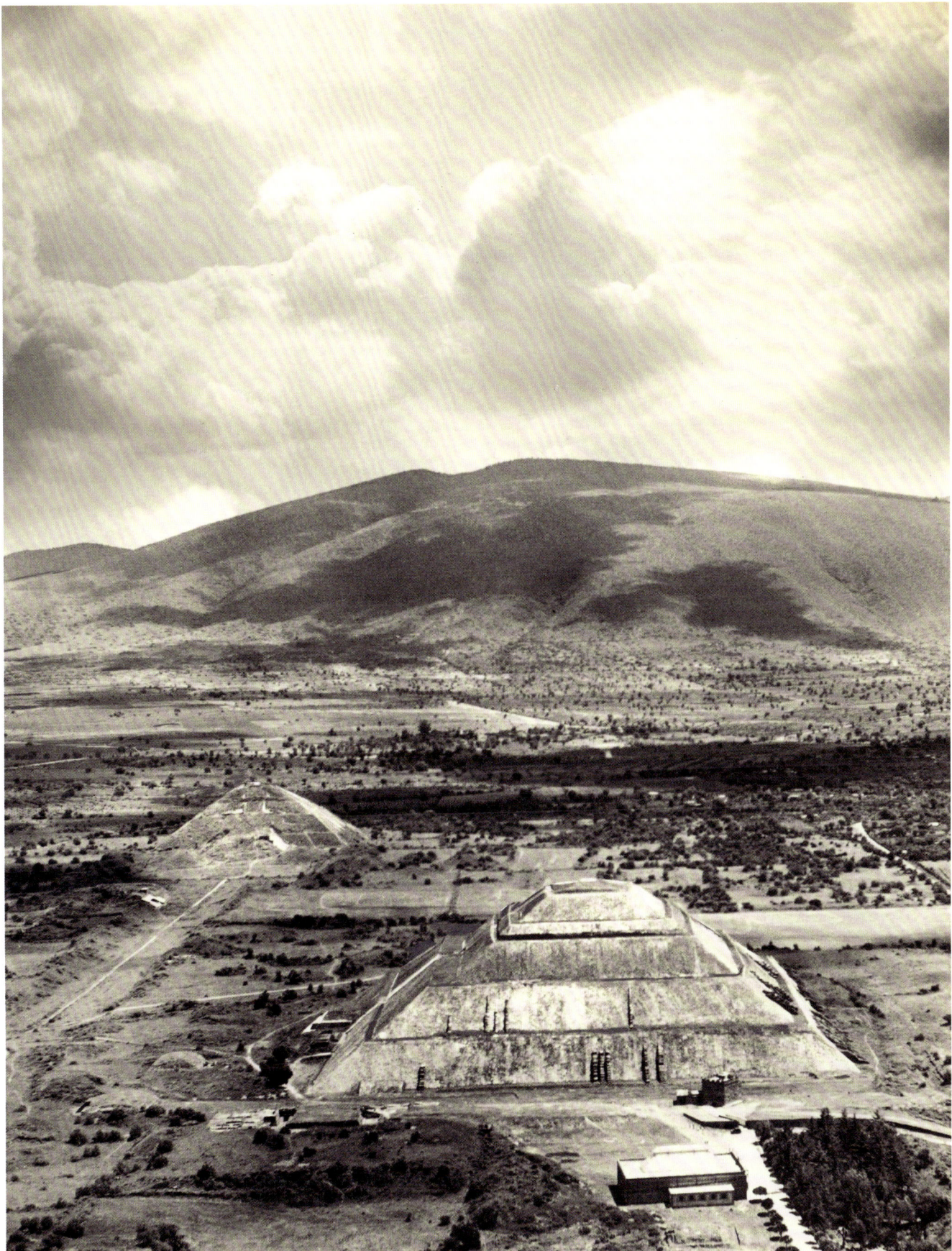

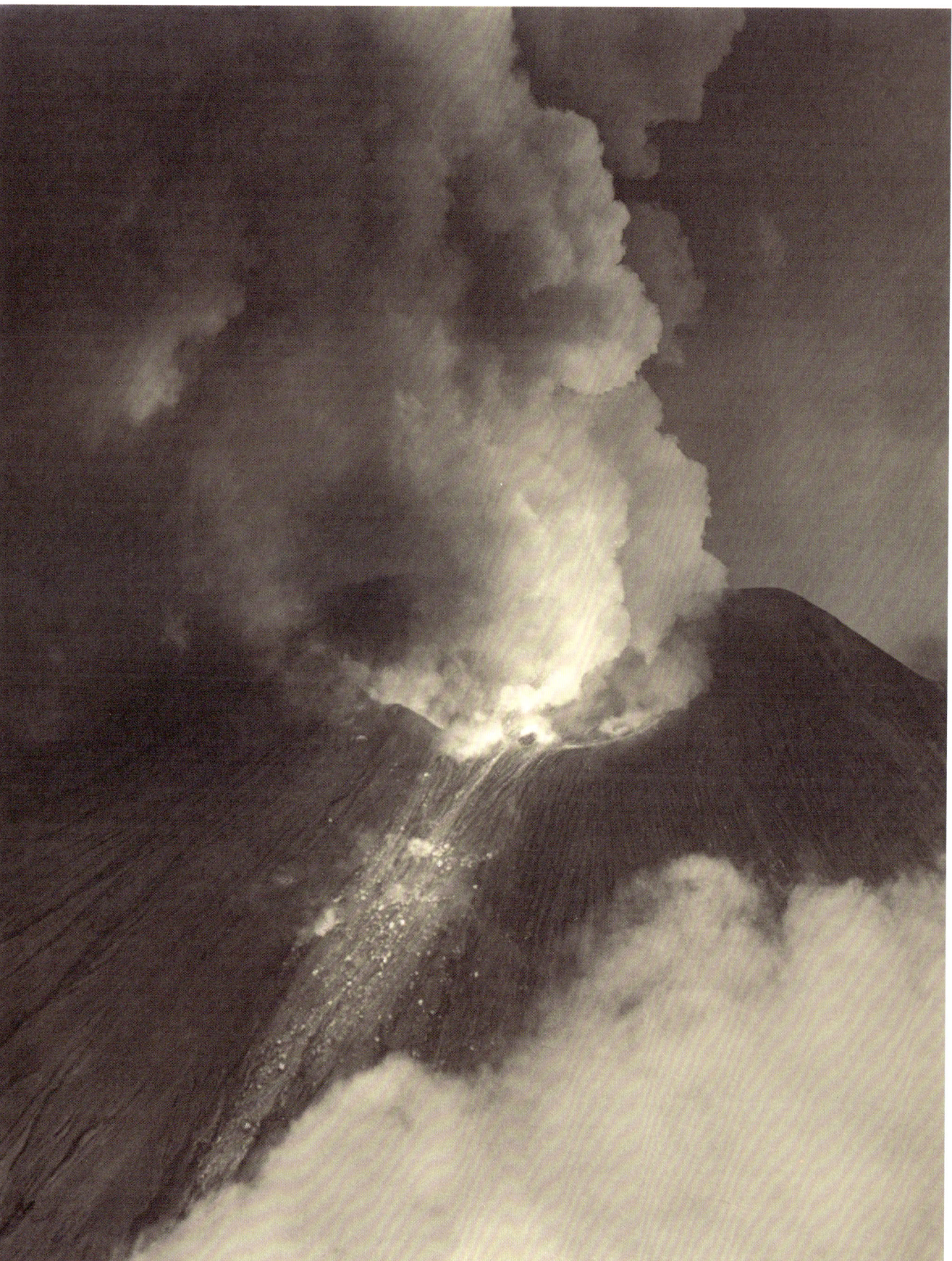

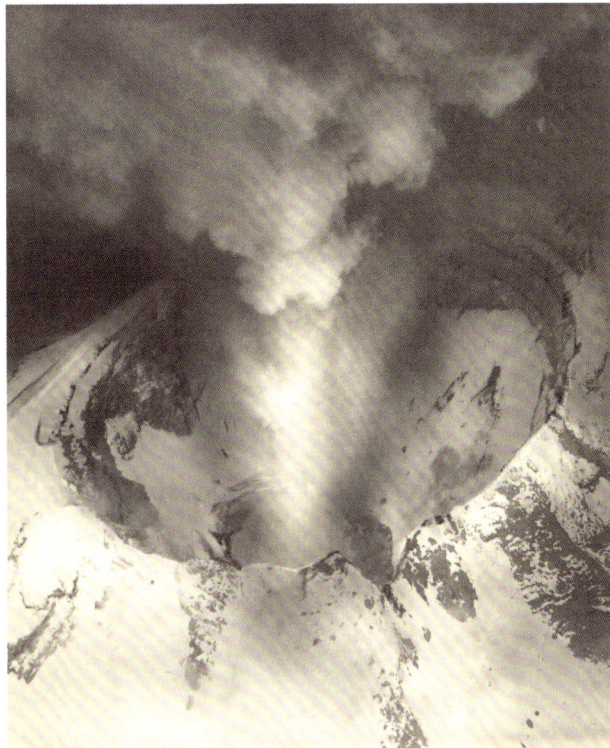

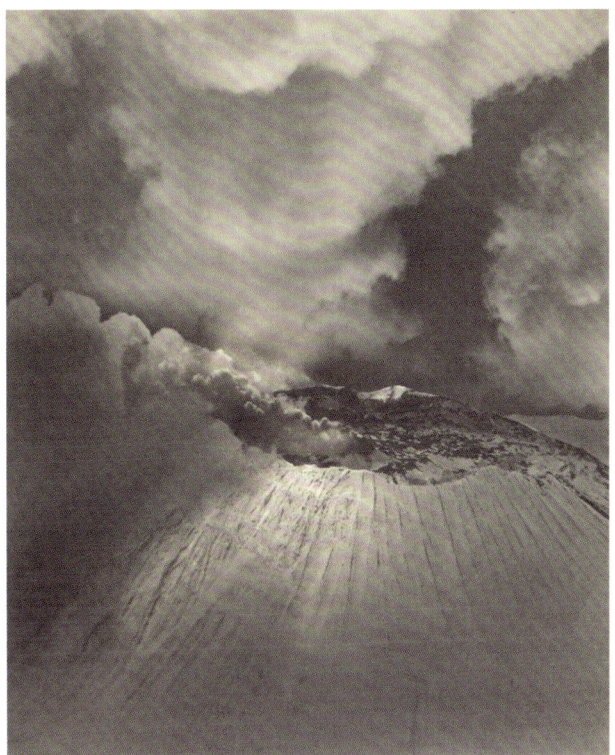

←
79. *Volcano. Santa María, Guatemala*, **1931, gelatin silver print, 46 × 38 cm.** National Galleries of Scotland. Purchased with Art Fund support, 2008

↑
80. *Volcano. Crater of Popocatépetl*, **1931, gelatin silver print, 45 × 38 cm.** National Galleries of Scotland. Purchased with Art Fund support, 2008

↗
81. *Volcano. Crater of Popocatépetl*, **1931, gelatin silver print, 46 × 38 cm.** National Galleries of Scotland. Purchased with Art Fund support, 2008

blowing across the vast amphitheatre, three-quarters-of-a-mile wide, struck the steep inner wall of the crater and steamed downward beneath the heated and lighter currents uprising. The passage across abounded in air pockets (so called) and cross currents which caused the aeroplane to proceed in a most uncertain manner. Beneath us the circular lake of boiling lava emitted numerous spouts of smoke and steam, whilst round its edge played occasional fires which, suddenly springing up and flickering awhile, as suddenly disappeared.[22]

Victorious, he headed for home:

And so back round the Gulf of Mexico to Brownsville in Texas, there to be closely examined by a very serious, cigar-smoking committee of Texans, and eventually re-admitted into the U.S.A as 'a perfect physical specimen, but deprived of speech.' Thus it was written. (And it was well worth while flying those thousands of miles just to be named in official language as 'a perfect physical specimen.')[23]

With this last great adventure under his belt, and now in his fifties, Buckham settled into a quieter pace of life. He died in Brighton at seventy-six, far exceeding the life expectancy predicted when he first took to the skies.

Afterword

THE CLOUD LIBRARY was carefully packed up by Buckham's son Stanley, to be stored alongside his archive of photographs, documents and camera equipment.

At the time of his death in 1956, Alfred Buckham was a respected aerial photographer, his images familiar to those interested in this area of photographic endeavour through a multitude of articles in popular magazines. In the interwar years, he had exhibited his photographs across Britain, with many of the prints still bearing the stamps of photographic society competitions from cities as far apart as Cambridge and Edinburgh. Despite winning medals, he never fully achieved the recognition as an artist that he sought from an early age.

Stanley had the foresight to know that this story didn't end with his father's death. He understood that it wasn't just the awe-inspiring photographs that would fascinate future generations of photographers and art enthusiasts but the unique way they were created. We have him to thank for retaining so much material from his father's darkroom.

I have had the pleasure of reading Buckham's letters, diaries, poetic musings and newspaper columns. Sitting in the quiet library at the Portrait Gallery in Edinburgh, I had to pause my research to explain to a colleague why I was chuckling to myself.

I recounted Buckham's latest scrape, a run-in with a 'cantankerous' bush following yet another spectacular crash. It is very rare that archive research gives such an insight into the personality and vision of the artist, or proves to be so entertaining.

Throughout his life, Stanley continued to advocate for his father's legacy. He undertook further research into his military and photographic career, and saw some of the photographs enter major museum collections, including that of the Metropolitan Museum of Art in New York. In 1990 the National Galleries of Scotland acquired Buckham's dazzling photograph of Edinburgh (32). This image inspired Celia Ferguson to track down Stanley and resulted in him supporting her to write *A Vision of Flight: The Aerial Photography of Alfred G. Buckham*, which was published in 2007 – a year after Stanley's death.

Buckham's archive is now in the care of his grandsons, Richard and John. In 2008, with assistance from Art Fund, the National Galleries of Scotland purchased a further group of twenty photographs that demonstrate Buckham's connection to Scotland. These photographs have since become hugely popular with visitors.

A few years ago, when researching transportation photographs for an upcoming exhibition, my colleague James Berry and I started to delve deeper

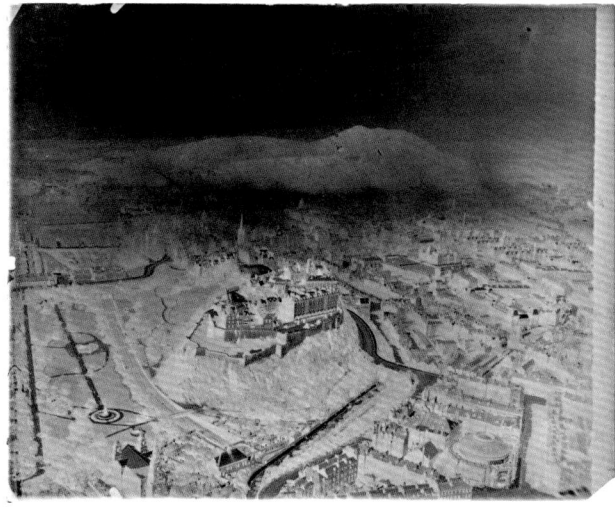

↑
82. *Edinburgh Castle, c.*1918, glass plate negative, 10 × 12.5 cm. National Galleries of Scotland. Purchased from Richard and John Buckham 2019

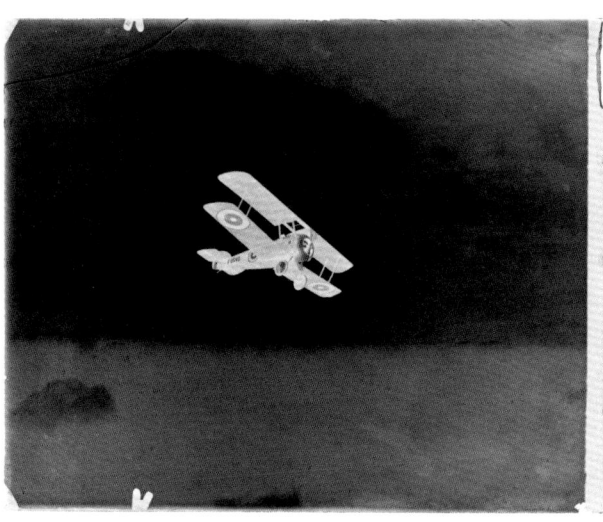

↑
83. *Aeroplane, c.*1918, glass plate negative, 10 × 12.5 cm. National Galleries of Scotland. Purchased from Richard and John Buckham 2019

into Buckham's photographic techniques. This led us to reconnect with the Buckham family and write an article exploring how the photographs were crafted. Prompted by the interest in this article, the National Galleries of Scotland purchased Buckham's camera (31) and part of his negative library, including the three glass plates used to make *Edinburgh* (32). I will never forget the sense of satisfaction I felt on eventually spotting the correct cloud formation after several days of sifting through thousands of negatives. These additions to the collection mean that we will always be able to tell Buckham's story, from his adventures in the air to his innovation in the darkroom.

For the exhibition *Alfred Buckham: Daredevil Photographer* the archive has been reunited. This accompanying publication is a lasting record of Buckham's remarkable life and his achievements as an artist. We are grateful to Richard and John for lending so generously to the exhibition and to the V&A for allowing us to show the key work *The Heart of the Empire* (28).

Buckham occupies an unusual position in photographic history. He was an analogue photographer with huge technical skill, following in the footsteps of the nineteenth-century photographers who invented composite photography to solve the conundrum of needing varying exposure times for different parts

of the landscape. In some ways he was actively old-fashioned – doggedly using glass plate negatives at a time when film was dominant.

His outlook, however, was very modern. The unique technique Buckham developed to craft his photographs – adding in different elements, blending and retouching – was a forerunner of contemporary photography. It is what digital photographers do in post-production and what can now be done in seconds in Photoshop and on social media. In this sense Buckham bridges the gap between photography's origins and how we experience it in the twenty-first century.

It is an interesting moment to view Buckham's photographs. Changing technology is making us question more than ever what is real. Buckham's pictures are a reminder that photography has never been 'true'. It has always pushed the boundaries of technology, seeking new and innovative ways to make images. As we navigate this confusing new era of image making, I look at these photographs and remember what makes great art – the human creativity and vision that Buckham had in abundance.

Louise Pearson
Curator of Photography
National Galleries of Scotland

Notes

All articles are by Alfred Buckham,
unless otherwise stated.

Introduction
1   'Pictorial photography in the skyway',
     Camera Craft, April 1937, pp.164–65.

In the Air
1   'Flying into the realm of the night', *New York
     Times Magazine*, 11 May 1930, p.9.
2   'Obituary. Alfred G. Buckham', *Photographic
     Journal*, April 1957, p.71.
3   Alfred Buckham's military records.
4   Ibid.
5   'Southward bound', *Fortune Magazine*,
     October 1931, p.72.
6   'Flying into the realm of the night', *New York
     Times Magazine*, 11 May 1930, p.17.
7   'Flying into the realm of the night', *Fortune
     Magazine*, October 1931, p.72.
8   'The Man and the print', *Amateur
     Photographer*, April 1928, p.339.
9   'Masters of photography: Captain A.G.
     Buckham', *Camera*, January 1927, p.354.
10   'Pictorial photography in the skyway',
     Camera Craft, April 1937, p.164.
11   Ibid., p.157.
12   'Pictorial photography in the skyway',
     Amateur Photographer, May 1929, p.26.
13   Ibid.
14   'Masters of photography: Captain A.G.
     Buckham', *Camera*, January 1927, p.354.
15   'Southward bound', *Fortune Magazine*,
     October 1931, p.72.
16   'London, rain and the "hoary Thames": a
     wonderful air view', *Illustrated London News*,
     12 September 1925, p.481.

In the Darkroom
1   'Masters of photography: Captain A.G.
     Buckham', *Camera*, January 1927, p.354.
2   'Pictorial photography in the skyway',
     Amateur Photographer, May 1929, p.26.
3   'Masters of photography: Captain A.G.
     Buckham', *Camera*, January 1927, p.354.
4   'A Flying photographer III: above volcanoes
     dead and alive', *Morning Post*, 12 January
     1934.
5   'Pictorial photography in the skyway',
     Camera Craft, April 1937, pp.164–65.
6   Ibid.

In Scotland
1   'The man & the print', *Amateur
     Photographer*, April 1928, p.339.
2   *'Where the duke "played in": the "Mecca" of
     golf from the air'*, *Illustrated London News*,
     4 October 1930, p.569.
3   *Tatler*, 14 January 1931, p.61.
4   'The Smoke fiend. Photographer's views on
     Scottish conditions. Flying over Edinburgh',
     Scotsman, 31 May 1935, p.7.
5   Ibid.

In the Americas
1   'A Flying photographer: record of an amazing
     19,000 miles' tour', *Morning Post*,
     15 December 1933.
2   'A Volcano from the air' and 'A Flying
     photographer: record of an amazing 19,000
     miles' tour', *Morning Post*, 3 and
     15 December 1933.
3   'A Flying photographer: record of an amazing
     19,000 miles' tour', *Morning Post*,
     15 December 1933.
4   Letter from Alfred Buckham to his son
     Stanley from RMS *Berengaria*, 14 April 1931.
5   'A Flying photographer: record of an amazing
     19,000 miles' tour', *Morning Post*,
     15 December 1933.
6   Ibid.
7   Buckham's journal from South America, 1931.
8   'A Flying photographer: record of an amazing
     19,000 miles' tour', *Morning Post*,
     15 December 1933.
9   'The Pan-American Air Mail crosses the
     Amazon', *Morning Post*, 9 December 1933.
10   *Morning Post*, 15 December 1933.
11   Ibid.
12   'A Flying photographer II: over the wall of the
     Andes', *Morning Post*, 29 December 1933.
13   Ibid.
14   'A Flying photographer III: above volcanoes
     dead and alive', *Morning Post*, 12 January
     1934.
15   Ibid.
16   Buckham's journal from South America, 1931.
17   'A flying photographer III: above volcanoes
     dead and alive', *Morning Post*, 12 January
     1934.
18   Ibid.
19   Ibid.
20   Ibid.
21   Ibid.
22   Ibid.
23   'A Flying photographer: record of an amazing
     19,000 miles' tour', *Morning Post*,
     15 December 1933.